ANSWERS
TO PRAYERS AND QUESTIONS ASKED ALONG THE WAY TO THE GRAVE

James Francis Dille

WESTBOW
PRESS®
A DIVISION OF THOMAS NELSON
& ZONDERVAN

Copyright © 2018 James Francis Dille.

All rights reserved. No part of this book may be used or reproduced by any means, graphic, electronic, or mechanical, including photocopying, recording, taping or by any information storage retrieval system without the written permission of the author except in the case of brief quotations embodied in critical articles and reviews.

This book is a work of non-fiction. Unless otherwise noted, the author and the publisher make no explicit guarantees as to the accuracy of the information contained in this book and in some cases, names of people and places have been altered to protect their privacy.

Scripture quotations marked (NLT) are taken from the Holy Bible, New Living Translation, copyright © 1996, 2004, 2007 by Tyndale House Foundation. Used by permission of Tyndale House Publishers, Inc., Carol Stream, Illinois 60188. All rights reserved.

WestBow Press books may be ordered through booksellers or by contacting:

WestBow Press
A Division of Thomas Nelson & Zondervan
1663 Liberty Drive
Bloomington, IN 47403
www.westbowpress.com
1 (866) 928-1240

Because of the dynamic nature of the Internet, any web addresses or links contained in this book may have changed since publication and may no longer be valid. The views expressed in this work are solely those of the author and do not necessarily reflect the views of the publisher, and the publisher hereby disclaims any responsibility for them.

Any people depicted in stock imagery provided by Getty Images are models, and such images are being used for illustrative purposes only.
Certain stock imagery © Getty Images.

ISBN: 978-1-9736-2104-1 (sc)
ISBN: 978-1-9736-2103-4 (hc)
ISBN: 978-1-9736-2105-8 (e)

Library of Congress Control Number: 2018902387

Print information available on the last page.

WestBow Press rev. date: 03/07/2018

Contents

Philosophy, Religion, and Me 1
Villa Ridge 3
The Essence of Christianity 5
Amazing Grace 8
Amendments to the Bible 10
And the Word Was Made Flesh 13
Anticipation, Experience, and Memory 16
Apologetics 20
Awareness 23
Betrayal 27
Boxes 31
Changes in Attitudes 35
Christian Churches 41
Christianity by the Cafeteria Plan 45
Death 48
Disagreement 52
Don't Worry; Be Happy 55
Small Straws in a Soft Wind, by Marsha Burns 57
Endings 59
Enlightenment 62
Fear 65
For the Love of God, Get Ready 69
For the Love of God 72
Friendship 76
God and Our Brain (Seeking Inner Peace) 79
Faith versus Intellect 83
Good Vibrations 87
Happiness and Unhappiness 90
Heaven 93
Here I Am, Lord 96
Humiliation 99

I'm Dreaming of a White Christmas	102
Islam or Christianity	105
Jesus: The Only Way	108
Lasting Friendships	111
Leadership	115
The Prayer of St. Francis	117
Listen to the Music	119
Love-Hate (Two Sides of the Same Issue)	122
Mary Mother of Jesus	126
Miracles Unrecognized	129
Moral Wisdom	133
Oldtown USA	136
Omega	140
Our Changing World	144
Please Validate Me	148
Pleasing God	151
Political Correctness versus Christian Correctness	155
Polls	159
Problem Solving	162
Solitude	166
Stillness	169
Stress	172
Thank You for Being My Friend	175
Thanks for the Memories	178
The Back Nine	181
The Church	185
The Devil Made Me Do It	190
The Final Answer (Or, What Was Your Question?)	193
The Land of the Discarded	196
The Last Great Generation?	200
The Most Important Decision You Can Make	203
The Power of the Spirit	207
My Prayer	211
The Ripple of Evil	212
The Root of All Evil	216
The Scriptures	219

The Spirit of Christmas: Christmas Past, Christmas Present, and
    Christmas Yet-to-Come 222
The Trinity.. 226
The Twilight Zone 229
To Thine Own Self Be True 233
Invictus 236
Trust and Faith 237
Unraveling Government, Politics, Religion, and Life...................... 240
What a Good Boy Am I (I'm a Better Christian than You) 245
What Can I Do.. 248
What Would You Like to Say to the Future World? 250
When to Stand up and When to Shut Up 253
Whose Fault Is It? 256
Whose Life Is It, Anyway?... 260
Why Be a Christian? 264
Why Bother?.. 268

Philosophy, Religion, and Me

There have been philosophers (those who tried to understand) since humankind developed consciousness, from Socrates to Immanuel Kant to Eric Hoffer. Even before the thoughts developed by these great minds, smaller minds tried to understand. Even my small mind seeks to understand where we fit in the universe. Some men trying to understand the writings of Kant would choose to take a walk alone in the woods in order to avoid madness. Hoffer thought that despots and fanatical cultural movements developed because of the absence of self-esteem and contentment. Kant thought that three philosophical approaches to understanding were from reason, experience, and somehow a transcendental understanding tying the other two together. Both drew upon Socrates's understanding of how knowledge is acquired and relates to truth.

Not pretending to understand much about life, I do understand that we're not all equipped with brains that support minds capable of this depth of thinking. Therefore, there are stair steps from great thinkers down to lesser thinkers. I believe the greatest mind is one that can produce understanding with the fewest words. The greatest of these was Jesus, who taught so the simplest mind could grasp his philosophy of love's omnipotence.

Understanding the concept of time has befuddled me since I was very young. I remember walking along a road as a ten-year-old, thinking that when I reached that rock up ahead of me, there would be a moment in time that would recede farther back with each step I took. There have been nearly seventy years and many steps from that rock that represented a point in time, and I am still befuddled. I see each of my friends and family who have died as rocks in the road of my time, which I continue to leave farther and farther back down the road. I remember seeing a video on TV of a herd of elephants walking around their matriarch, who had died. They paused, as if trying to understand and show some respect, and then continued on down the trail. We do the same as we try to appreciate something we really don't understand and then continue on down the trail of our lives. Immanuel Kant filled many pages in his *Critique of Pure Reason,* attempting to explain his system of principles. He didn't do a good enough job and used too many words for my poor intellect to absorb.

Understanding how the human mind ponders and produces thoughts is of great value to our transcendental development of understanding. It is of little value, however, unless we realize that we can never completely understand the omnipotence and omnipresence of God. We are asked to utilize faith when understanding fails.

I have attempted, with my thoughts and writings, to be perhaps the bottom step on the ladder of thoughts belonging to similar minds. Through logic, experience, and mostly faith, I believe that God not only exists, he exists in me and you.

I pray that my writings will have a place in your quest for understanding by filling gaps previously filled with faith, thereby making their faith stronger and more productive.

Villa Ridge

Villa Ridge, Illinois, was more than a village when I passed through on my brief journey toward adulthood. Villa Ridge was a living, breathing thing, akin to a human. As with a human, there were levels of intricacy working together while not being understood by most contributors. Each of us have contradicting parts woven together closely; sometimes unaware of the presence of other parts or their importance for our wholeness. So it was with my little town. We had intelligence of varying levels, as well as ignorance hanging about, preventing understanding at a higher level. We had saints, undeclared and often unrecognized. We also had evil, but evil only fed on the absence of love. Dangerous microbes can colonize in our bodies, but they are held at bay by antibodies; a similar self-controlling wisdom guided by love, prevailed in Villa Ridge.

There was an awareness of the presence of the creator, which held us together in a moral sense, even if he was not always venerated. If I think of my town being a human, it was someone with a permanent smile on its face. It was a human made of good stuff and acting in a mostly loving manner while being unaware of its own goodness. It was of a human likeness that made one proud to have been produced from its loins. As a young man, I thought that other towns were equally loving and nurturing, but I've discovered we were somewhat unique. Not perfect by any means; we suffered bigotry, even racism, but learned as we grew, like most people do. We learned that love overcomes selfishness, fear, ignorance, as well as all things evil. I loved this little town, which nurtured me through the good, the bad, and the ugly.

Just like a person, my little village grew up, matured, suffered at times, but endured, until it was no longer needed as a physical being. Even though death takes much, it cannot take away love. Fortified by this love and understanding its source is our Lord Jesus; I attempt with this book to help others find the love Jesus brought to this earth.

I dedicate this book to the people of Villa Ridge.

The Essence of Christianity

Question: What do you think the essence of Christianity really is?

There is a man at my church who displays the essence of Christianity in its purest form. I am sorry to say that I don't even know his name. We often refer to him as "the 'How you' man" because of his sincere greeting to all. This man doesn't seem aware of race, wealth, or intellect. One thing he is aware of is his love for God and all who come across his path. My heart is warmed and eyes made misty not only from his greeting, but also when he has to leave early because of his ride. When he leaves, he waves goodbye to the pastor. Then he gives us all a wave with a smile as he walks down the aisle. When we ushers pass the collection plate, he rises and digs into his pocket until he comes up with whatever coins he has, and then he deposits them without considering any shame or pride in the amount.

Something about this pure Christian man fills my heart, as he feels no embarrassment when he boldly blesses all of us fumbling Christians. This sweet man is unaware of his goodness and how it opens up hearts in ways the most eloquent speaker could not. I sense something pure in this humble man—something that makes me want to jump up and shout, "Glory to God!" But I don't; I just sit there, afraid to express my love in such a bold way. I wonder if we fail to understand that if Jesus were to bless us with his presence in a visible form, he would do it in this very manner. He has done it; this wonderful man's presence each Sunday is the essence of Jesus in our midst. We all should be shouting with joy.

Jesus is with each of us—every day, every second. He is shouting above our heads as we blunder through our lives, not paying attention. Most of us who profess to love Jesus pass him in some manner each day, without notice. We just pass him by because we have things to attend to. We expect him to come with a roar of thunder and bright, flashing lights. That would not be his way; he would just appear among us in different forms, waiting for us to offer love. I don't think Jesus is returning; I think he never left. He has remained in our presence in many humble forms we are too proud to kneel to.

I often think of the janitor of our little church when I grew up. Ol' Charley was a very quiet and unassuming gentleman; this poor old man usually had coal dust on his face. He took care of many mundane tasks in our community, without notice by most. I remember one evening when our pastor asked for testimonies from the congregation. The usual suspects all stood and went on and on about their relationship with Christ, while Charley stood quietly in the back row.

Finally, the preacher asked, "Charley, do you have something to say?"

Charley stood. In a quiet, completely unpretentious voice, he told about his thankfulness for all God had blessed him with. His simple eloquence made all of us feel the presence of Jesus in our midst. His was the last testimony that evening.

I believe we should begin each day with a few minutes recognizing Jesus's presence. We must feel the love he offers and take that love with us the remainder of the day. Life is much fuller when you can see Jesus in everyone, even in the humblest of our brethren.

If we continually see Jesus throughout each day, we will become more like him. We will become the essence of Christ.

"We know how much God loves us, and we have put our trust in him. God is love, and all who live in love live in God, and God lives in them. And as we live in God, our love grows more perfect. So we will not be afraid on the Day of Judgment, but we can face him with confidence because we are like Christ here in this world" (1 John 4:16–17).

"So be sure to pay attention to what you hear. To those who are open to my teaching, more understanding will be given. But to those who are not listening, even what they think they have will be taken away from them" (Luke 8:18).

1. Have you ever felt like you failed to see Jesus?
2. If Jesus were to visit your church in a physical form, how would you expect him to appear?
3. Do you understand you fail to see Jesus when you fail to help the poorest of the poor?
4. If an unclean old man came into your church, would you ask him to leave?
5. If you have nothing but love, are you richer that the one who has nothing but money?
6. Do you give as much as you can to your church and charity?

"The law holds man in bondage; love makes him free."—Ludwig Feuerbach, *The Essence of Christianity*

Amazing Grace

Question: How do you handle it when someone insults you?

We Christians often think that we need to do good things and help others so that we can gain entrance to heaven. In our subconscious minds, we think God loves us because we are good people who do good deeds. We think that if we do a lot of work at our churches, God will see that, and we will be given eternal life with our Lord Jesus. Some people think that they can gain the attention of the Lord by giving more money to their churches or to charity. "Well, I'm not like that," you may say. "But the fact that I visit people in the nursing home each week and cook Thanksgiving dinner at the rescue mission every year makes me a pretty good Christian."

Some may take the opposite position and say, "I don't do much at all. I go to church a couple times a year, but I seldom do much for anyone in need. I'm kind of a lukewarm Christian."

We all have those thoughts at times and wonder if we are doing enough to make it. Then when someone dies, we often place a score upon the life that person led. We think, *Well, that person didn't do much at all to gain heaven in their life.*

We all insult God on a daily basis. Not many of us lead lives like saints, but we figure we are about as good as anybody else, so God probably will let us into heaven when we die. *If he let old man Smith in, who sinned most of his life—and the preacher praised so much at his service because he asked for forgiveness on his last day—he will surely give me a pass.*

We all miss the same thing the Pharisees missed in Jesus's time. We think that a life lived pretty well compared to others should be rewarded in the next life if we rack up enough points and go to church regularly. If we make the proper sacrifice and follow all the rules, we will make it, just like the Pharisees thought they would. Sometime in the Middle Ages, the Catholic church came up with plenary indulgences, relieving devotees of some of their temporal punishment for sins already forgiven by fasting, giving alms, and prayer. They even assigned points (years) for each act.

Grace means getting something that you do not deserve: unmerited favor. We don't get to heaven because we earn it. We get to heaven because of the grace of our Lord. It is a gift. Jesus was sacrificed on the cross so that all who believe would be eligible to receive eternal life.

"For God loved the world so much that he gave his one and only Son, that everyone who believes in Him shall not perish but have eternal life" (John 3:16).

"For by works of the law no human being will be justified in his sight since through the law comes knowledge of sin. But now the righteousness of God has been manifested apart from the law, although the Law and the Prophets bear witness to it—the righteousness of God faith in Jesus Christ for all who believe. For there is no distinction: for all have sinned and fall short of the glory of God, and are justified by his grace as a gift, through the redemption that is in Christ Jesus" (Romans 3:20–24).

1. Does this mean that none of us deserve reward by our own merit? Why or why not?
2. Why do you think God gives the same gift to someone who was late coming to the Lord?
3. Do you ever thank God for his grace or just expect it because you have lived a good life?
4. Have you known someone which was not a Christian until the very end?
5. What do you think God expects of you?

Amendments to the Bible

Question: If the prophets and saints suggested a method to amend the Bible, as the founding fathers of the United States arranged for its Constitution, what amendment would you like to make?

I doubt there are many of us who want to be condemned by our scriptures, friends, or government for our behavior. Most people want to be like children and do whatever they want. Like children, many try to hide bad behavior from their parents, teachers, friends, and even God. If we cannot hide our questionable behavior, we try to justify it. "My dad does it, my brother does it, and everyone does it." We sometimes justify our behavior by saying, "I was hungry, so I ate my sister's piece of pie." When children have bodily cravings, they justify unacceptable behavior in their minds until they are taught differently. Adults try to justify certain sexual activities in the same way, saying, "I have these feelings that I cannot control," "I was born with certain feelings," or "A lot of people do it."

America's founding fathers made it very difficult to amend the US Constitution, because they knew over time, it would lose its original intent if each generation was allowed to amend it; they knew it would not take long for our nation to disappear—and take the high ideals it originally represented with it. There are some citizens today who want the Constitution to be a living document that can be interpreted differently by judges.

I believe if our scriptures are in essence amended by contemporary mores and values, Christianity will not survive. It appears to me that we are acting in the same manner as secular judges when dominations or individuals ignore certain biblical teachings or apply interpretations other than those inspired by God. Either we do not think the Bible to be important for the survival of Christianity, or we think the authors were not inspired by God. Perhaps we think the Bible should be a living document that can be interpreted by current standards.

All people have desires, feelings, and cravings that are difficult to control. People in the United States are obese because they do not exercise and cannot control their food intake. We sometimes have affairs with another's spouse or desire too much wine or narcotics. Some people think that the desire to have sexual relations with anyone should not be condemned.

There are some people in our country today who believe we should not have national borders. They are globalists. There are many different cultures in our diverse states making civil laws that do not consider these differences; therefore, creating one world government seems implausible until the world accepts Christ.

Laws are necessary for any society to function. Civil law in the United States is based upon our Constitution, which is based upon Judeo-Christian principles, which is to say it is based on the Bible. We are not allowed to decide which laws we want to abide by. We are required under threat of punishment to abide by all laws. Likewise, our sacred scriptures do not allow us to decide to follow some of the teachings while ignoring others. Loud voices to the contrary do not change truth.

If we all decide to only follow certain civil laws, or if we decide not to have borders, we will cease to have a country. By the same token, if we decide some of the teachings of Christ's New Testament are archaic and need to be ignored or amended, Christianity will cease to exist. Today, some want truth to be altered to suit their behavior instead of trying to control their behavior to suit God.

I have noticed that the modern affirmation of faith in the Methodist hymnal even fails to affirm our faith in the Bible (although the Korean affirmation of faith in the same hymnal makes this affirmation of sacred scriptures clearly).

The change in the truth seen by Pilate, which resulted in the Crucifixion of Jesus, was because he listened to loud voices.

"But the crowd shouted louder and louder for Jesus's death, and their voices prevailed" (Luke 23:23).

1. Are we allowing loud voices to change our faith in the truth of our Bible?
2. Do you disagree with any teachings in the New Testament?
3. What do you think the loud voices are calling for today?
4. Have you ever justified your bad behavior by thinking, *This is a different time*?
5. We are sometimes drawn away from truth by quiet voices that multiply; do you see that happening in your church?
6. Do you ever think loud voices are taking our country in a direction away from God?
7. Do you ever fail to speak up for Christianity because of political correctness (PC)?
8. I can think of at least three clear directives in our New Testament we ignore today. Marriage is between one man and one woman, we should not divorce, and homosexual activity is wrong; can you think of more?

Your loud voice is not proof of the depth of your knowledge, for an empty box makes more noise than a full one.

And the Word Was Made Flesh

Question: Can you remember a family Easter when you were young?

I just experienced a wonderful weekend, starting with Good Friday and ending late Easter Sunday.

The family began to arrive at my home and at the cabin on Friday evening. The children were filled with anticipation and excitement for the celebration to come. My daughter Ashley and husband Ryan, along with two dogs, as well as two grandchildren were waiting at my home when I arrived after a day some might describe as work. I tend to do more work trying to avoid work than I produce these days. Of course, March Madness was beginning, and the men tried to get a glance now and then to see if our favorite team was surviving. The next morning, old Grandpa began a ritual with the seven-year-old granddaughter and the four-year-old grandson of making biscuits. I usually have adults standing around to grab the milk or flour before it gets scattered, but this day, the adults scattered. Alone with the adventure, I tried to plan each step in a way that would produce less stress. It seemed the only one that got stressed was this grandfather. I had to sit a while and let my spinning head slow down and turn the rest of breakfast preparation to my daughter. We all soon had a great time and enjoyed breakfast together.

In the afternoon, we gathered at our place on the river to eat barbeque and fly kites. My son arranged chairs in the field and provided kites for anyone healthy enough to chase one. Ol' Granddad found a comfortable lawn chair and enjoyed the fun and laughter only happy kids produce. Soon, the adults were giving instructions and running to gather enough wind to get a kite into the air. Some failed, but others had some success looking for the wind, which seemed to disappear. Kids, dogs, moms, dads, cousins all excitedly tried to outdo each other. Later, all who were brave enough got to shoot a rifle at a stump in the river. The joy of that small point of time produced memories to exceed most great moments. Enjoy the small things now because they will be the big things you remember in a few years.

Easter Sunday morning, our family filled one whole pew, only missing a few, and then we went home to the smell of baking ham and fixings. The pastor's message was placed somewhere in our mind to be called upon as wisdom in the future. The hunt for Easter eggs was a mix of screams and laughter as usual, as the bigger cousins kept watch over the smaller ones.

All of a sudden, everyone began to pack for the trip home, and it fell silent. Too silent. As I sat pondering the whole experience, I prayed that the cousins and their parents had bonded enough to want to hold on to the joy of family, not knowing that time would scatter us and the Lord would take some of us home. It may take an effort to stay in touch among those who are scattered by time and circumstance. But the seemingly small things they enjoyed that weekend would slowly grow into the big things they will cherish and want to hold on to.

God the Father came into this world in the flesh to teach us. We try to make his lesson complicated, but it is really simple. We try to teach our children all about life, while they teach us what life is all about. It is about love.

"In the beginning the Word already existed. He was with God, and he was God. He was in the beginning with God. He created everything there is. Nothing exists that he didn't make. Life itself was in him, and this life gives light to everyone. The light shines through the darkness, and the darkness can never extinguish it" (John 1:1–5).

Enjoy the little things in life, for one day you will look back and realize they were really the big things.

1. Have you ever been so busy filming an event that you missed it?
2. Why do people sometimes have to lose something before they appreciate what they had?
3. Did the apostles follow the same mistake when they lost Jesus until the Holy Spirit came upon them?
4. Why do we venerate the cross more than the empty tomb?

Anticipation, Experience, and Memory

Question: Can you think of an experience in your life that lived up to the anticipation and has blended into a memory that has held fast in your truth?

I had a long conversation with my daughter last night about this subject. We talked about the value associated with anticipation and experience. Is anticipation more important than experience, or does memory have more value while living your life? The event itself is something we try to grasp as it flows by, but it is a slippery thing to hold on to, because when you become aware of something taking place, it has already slipped into the past. This subject is perhaps so esoteric you may not even want to ponder it, thinking, *What in the world does this have to do with the price of a Christmas tree?*

Can you remember that wonderful time of anticipation most of us experienced in the Decembers of our youth? The fragrances we associated with the season? Cedar, oranges, tangerines? Then the sounds of bells, carols, and happy voices. The morning of Christmas would often exceed our expectations because of the feeling of love, security, and family. We now have wonderful memories to savor that are released by a fragrance or sound.

One of my favorite stories is *A Christmas Carol*, about an old man who has become so self-centered that he has forgotten the real meaning of life. Old Ebenezer Scrooge is confronted by three ghosts one Christmas Eve night, which bring the past and the future into the present. Scrooge finds the lost values he once possessed and practiced. He was then forced to compare these with the nihilistic life he was living. The result was a renewal and an abrupt change for a better life. He was able to utilize memory to better see his failure and create or anticipate a better future. We do not need the ghosts of Christmas past, present, and yet to come to appear to us. If we will only find truth in self-analysis and seek guidance from the Lord, whose birth we are celebrating. When we do this and take the time to reflect and analyze events in the past and set goals based upon values of Christ, we will find real meaning in our lives.

We get caught up in the wonderful feeling we get when we give gifts at Christmastime. This is good; however, have you ever thought about giving yourself to someone by engaging in a thoughtful conversation? A conversation evolves, asking questions and becoming really interested in the answers. Sometimes, you wait while the other party speaks so you can think of a story to top theirs. Have you ever noticed that you seldom have much one-on-one time with your children or grandchildren? You arrange time for friends more often than you do for family. You enjoy big celebrations with family, involving anticipation, experience, and created memories, but it takes more effort to spend alone time with a grandson or granddaughter. You even find it difficult to spend alone time with your spouse, preferring instead to watch the TV or read the newspaper. When was the last time you really looked at your spouse and had a conversation? A time when you turned off the TV, folded your newspaper, or closed your book so that you could concentrate on her or him? You may anticipate a football game and love watching each play and then talking about it later with your friends. How often do you think about what to talk about with your spouse? Do you really put yourself into experiencing a good talk with him or her? Then after that conversation, do you remember what was said? So often, we men only listen long enough to criticize something she said.

If you have more than one grandchild, it is a challenge to find those moments to really look into their eyes while listening to their thoughts, experiences, and desires. While listening to our eight-year-old granddaughter and five-year-old grandson, they often bang me on the head with a plastic toy. It takes effort and planning to find something to do with one grandchild at a time that will make them remember a one-on-one experience with Grandpa or Grandma.

There are many prophecies about Jesus in the Old Testament, but this one is about anticipation:

"All right then, the Lord himself will choose the sign. Look! The virgin will conceive a child! She will give birth to a son and will call him Immanuel—God is with us" (Isaiah 7:14).

Then there is prophecy about what he will experience in Isaiah 53:3–7: "Yet it was our weaknesses he carried: it was our sorrows that weighed him down. Wounded and crushed for our sins. He was beaten that we might have peace. He was whipped, and we were healed! All of us have strayed away like sheep. We have left God's paths to follow our own. Yet the Lord laid on him the guilt and sins of us all."

We are taught, again in the Old Testament, why we should remember:

"You must read this law to all the people of Israel when they assemble before the Lord your God at the place he chooses. Call them all together—men, women, children, and the foreigners living in your towns—so they may listen and learn to fear the Lord your God and carefully obey all the terms of this law. Do this so that your children who have not known these laws will hear them and will learn to fear the Lord your God. Do this as long as you live in the land you are crossing the Jordan to occupy" (Deuteronomy 31:11–13).

1. We are told about the anticipation of the coming, what would happen and why we should remember. Have you studied and taught as we are admonished to do?
2. Have you ever acted like old Ebenezer Scrooge at Christmastime? Perhaps you get tired of the Christmas music?
3. Have you ever been stingy with your money? How about your time? Your home? Do you entertain friends or people who are alone at Christmas?

4. Do you know it took all three things anticipation, experience, and memory, for even the apostles to understand who and what Jesus was?
5. How can you make the spirit of Christmas last all year?
6. Have you ever shared Christ's love with a stranger? Did they enjoy talking to you?

Apologetics

Question: Is there anything that you feel confident enough in your skills or knowledge to teach others?

My wife's Bible study group is starting a study about Christian apologetics. As Mary worked on her studies, she asked me if I knew what apologetics was, and I had to admit that I did not. I looked up the definition and learned that it is the discipline of defending a position (often religious) through the systematic use of information. In our discussion, Mary told me that she understood it to mean that she was going to learn how to argue about Christianity, and she did not like to argue about religion. Most of us probably feel the same way.

I often think about a man I knew years ago and considered a friend; he was agnostic, at best. He told me that he was raised a Christian and had faith as a young man until he went away to college. His roommate was an intellectual of sorts and did not believe in God. My friend was unequipped to defend his faith with the seemingly logical arguments his roommate put forth, and he lost all faith as a result. My friend retired and moved away a few years ago, and I seldom heard from him again, until he unexpectedly came to our home one day for a visit. I was intrigued by the fact that when he sat down during our visit, our little dog, who loved everyone, tucked her tail and slipped away. I noticed in the paper that he died about a year or so ago and prayed that he rediscovered his faith before leaving this life.

During our entire life, we should be learners rather than learned. The philosopher Eric Hoffer once said, "In times of change, learners inherit the earth, while the learned find themselves beautifully equipped to deal with a world that no longer exists." Although Hoffer described himself as an atheist, he gives Christians good advice if we apply this to learning more about our faith. If we do not continue to equip our faith with information, we may someday be presented with arguments that defeat that faith. Throughout our lives, we should continue to educate ourselves in all ways, or the world will pass us by. We are becoming more aware of this fact by the technology developments that many refuse to try to learn about and utilize in their daily lives.

"Every human being is born on our planet with only the potential to become capable, not with the capabilities themselves" (H. S. Glenn, J. Nelsen. *Raising Self-Reliant Children in a Self-Indulgent World,* p. 48). We hopefully learn from our predecessors to equip ourselves to deal with the world, but we have the potential to develop and extend our knowledge to a point that we can become teachers. We go to church and Bible study in order to strengthen our faith but also to understand our faith enough to be able to defend and teach it. If you do not understand something well enough to teach others, then perhaps you do not understand it as well as you thought.

I often remember the Boy Scout promise: "I promise to keep myself physically strong, mentally awake, and morally straight." Paul reminds us of these things in his letter to Timothy:

"Do not waste time arguing over godless ideas and old wives' tales. Spend your time and energy in training yourself for spiritual fitness. Physical exercise has some value, but spiritual exercise is much more important, for it promises a reward in both this life and the next. This is true, and everyone should accept it. We work hard and suffer much in order that people will believe the truth, for our hope is in the living God who's the Savior of all people, and particularly of those who believe.

"Teach these things and insist that everyone learn them. Don't let anyone think less of you because you are young. Be an example to all believers in what you teach, in the way you live, in your love, your faith, and your purity. Until I get there, focus on reading the Scriptures to the church, encouraging the believers and teaching them" (1 Timothy 4:7–16).

1. Are you staying strong physically, mentally, and spiritually? Many of us spend a lot of time trying to stay physically strong, but do we spend enough time learning about our faith?
2. Do you ever read opposing ideas or listen to people without faith in order to strengthen your own ability to teach them? Do you sometimes feel unequipped to defend your faith?
3. Can you think of someone you know who needs you to help them in their faith?
4. What was the last book you read? Do you spend more time reading the sports page in the paper than your Bible?
5. Have your children or grandchildren ever taught you or reminded you anything about being a good Christian?
6. When you clean your car, it doesn't stay clean long; why do you think you can clean your spirit once and keep it clean?

Awareness

Question: Can you think of something you were not aware of or didn't appreciate as a child that you learned to enjoy as an adult?

Some of us walk around every day in a cloud that prevents us from being aware of our ability to control our mind. We seldom think about our spirit and its connectivity to everything. We think about our body more often, because it hurts, it is hungry, we think it is unattractive, or perhaps we think it is beautiful. We are often told today to at least be aware of our surroundings, look out for the boogie bears that are trying to hurt us. We are told to look out for bad drivers, avoid dangerous places, avoid substances and foods that may harm our bodies, and so on. I asked a friend if she tried to be aware of her world and she responded, "If I'm not aware of some things, I am not aware of what they are." Maybe that is our problem; we don't open our five senses to understand and appreciate what is around us. We are so busy worrying and thinking about ourselves and perceived problems, we don't see, hear, smell, touch, or taste the wonderful world and the people who live in it as well. That fact is why we have so many problems.

Several years ago, we took a trip to the country that was then named Yugoslavia. It was the year after the Winter Olympics were held in Sarajevo. It was a beautiful country, and the people we met were all very kind and helpful. Some of the Americans in our group, however, were so into themselves, they embarrassed the rest of us, including our three couples. They demanded attention and service that made us think of the phrase "the Ugly American."

We stayed in a ski lodge along with people from France and Germany. On the first morning, we assembled for our free breakfast and were a little surprised at our European food. There were hard rolls and cold cuts, hard boiled eggs, some kind of pickled fish, and other foods unfamiliar to us. We accepted the fare, becoming aware we were in a different country. We looked forward at least to a good cup of hot coffee, thinking that would be something like home. We were again surprised by the coffee, which was strong but lukewarm. This was unacceptable to one of our ladies, and she asked for some hot water to dilute and heat up her unfamiliar cup of brew. The waiter was very kind and brought all of us a little tea cup of very hot water. We asked him how to say hot water in his language so that we could ask in other places. He responded, "*Hase wasser*," or so we thought. Someone said, "That sounds like German, not whatever the Yugoslavs spoke."

Armed with our only learned phrase in the local language, we went to several restaurants during our tour, using it when we were served the same lukewarm brew. The reaction was always the same with each waiter. They looked shocked, embarrassed, and usually angry. Someone again mentioned it sounded like German and maybe they are still angry at Germans for their actions during World War II. It was several years later when I was telling a German lady who had married into our family, our experiences in Yugoslavia that I learned a lesson about being aware when someone is teaching me something. I told my German sister-in-law the phrase we had used to order hot water: Hase wasser. She laughed hysterically for a while and then corrected me: "No, no, no. You should have said, '*Heibes wasser*.' What you were using was German for sure, but it meant rabbit urine. When you pointed to your bad coffee, saying, 'Hase wasser,' you were telling your waiter your coffee tasted like rabbit urine."

You would think we would be very careful about speaking "their language" when visiting another country; however, my sweet wife failed again in Mexico when she tried to tell her maid that her shower had cold water. Instead of explaining to our maid that the water was cold, the perplexed little maid heard the American lady tell her there were cold beans in our shower. Now when we visit other nationalities, we depend upon those people understanding English.

We Americans too often expect to see, hear, smell, taste, and feel things in foreign countries like we do in our own country. We sometimes don't try to see the beauty God has blessed other places in the world with; we want things we do not understand to all be pleasing to our senses by demanding things to be changed to be like home. When we make our demands in their language, we should at least be sure that we are speaking it correctly.

We should try to be aware of everything we experience in this world and be thankful for being able to experience it, whether it's big things like love, liberty, mountains, or poetry or the more mundane things like a good cup of coffee or a hot shower. Awareness of our Lord should be the first thing we consider as we begin each day.

In Thornton Wilder's play *Our Town,* the character named Emily, having been given one day to return to the world after her death, calls out, "Goodbye Grover's Corners—Ma and Papa. Goodbye to clocks ticking—and my butternut tree!—and Mama's sunflowers—and food and coffee—and new-ironed dresses and hot baths—and sleeping and waking up! Oh earth, you're too wonderful for anyone to realize you! Do any human beings ever realize life while they live it—every, every minute?"

"Since everything God created is good, we should not reject any of it. We may receive it gladly, with thankful hearts" (1 Timothy 4:4–5).

1. Do you believe the Bible instructs us to reject this world and everything in it?
2. Do you think we are taught to look at the bad things in this world by the news and get in a habit of ignoring the goodness all around us?
3. Do you try to understand and appreciate other cultures and languages?
4. Who do you think is more aware: someone in jungles of Borneo, or an American?

5. Awareness includes different foods. Do you refuse to eat anything new or different?
6. Awareness should mainly be trying to be awake as we live life. If we are always trying to find things to complain about, can we be truly awake and aware?
7. Why do we relate worldliness to rejecting God instead of seeing the beauty in the world as loving God?

Betrayal

Question: Have you ever felt betrayed, by a spouse, a friend, a coworker, a boss, the government? Would you use a different term, perhaps "let down"?

Betrayal is a strong word, among many phrases we use casually today because television has taken the sting out of words. When we hear words constantly, they seem to lose some of their shock. *Liar* was at one time a word that might bring on a challenge to a dual, but the political dialog we are confronted with today uses *liar* so frequently, it has little value even when true.

My first memory of feeling betrayed was in the second grade. My friend Steve told the teacher something that I had told him my mom had said at dinner the night before. I had left the classroom for a few minutes, and when I returned, Ms. Beulah was red in the face and standing before my desk.

"Jimmy Dille," she said, "Steve tells me your mother thinks I am getting too old to be teaching. Well you tell your mother that if she thinks she can do a better job, come on down and give it a try."

I took care of the resentment I felt for Steve on the way home after school. Steve was a little overweight and made a wonderful sight and sound when I pushed him down a hill covered with thorn bushes. I remember hearing him say, "I'm sorry," as he rolled through the sticker bushes. I guess I forgave him because we remained friends all through school and adult life, until his death a few years ago. I miss him a great deal.

Our tongues can often result in the betrayal of loved ones and friends. We get so caught up in gossip as entertainment, we often fail to think about how passing along little things will have an effect on people's lives. Most of us go by the idea that if we did not start the gossip, then it's not wrong if the gossip is true. The biggest factor leading to betrayal is lack of faith. The foundation of faith is trust, and too often, we sinners do not trust ourselves, our friends, and our Lord. Instead of seeking ways to build trust and faith in ourselves, friends, and God, we seek ways to build ourselves up. We mistakenly think if we puff ourselves up, we will be more important in our own eyes and in the eyes of our friends and God. In the process of puffing ourselves up, we want to bring others down by our words and actions. Our misguided mind thinks we can elevate our stature by lowering the stature of others.

I recently attended a funeral of Bill, someone who was a casual friend in years past. Our friendship had suffered because I felt he had betrayed Tom, another mutual friend, years ago with his tongue because of what seemed to be selfish ambition. The result was Tom's career was destroyed. It was all about money and standing in our community. The trust between these two individuals failed, and Bill and Tom both suffered because of lost faith in each other. It doesn't really matter so much who was right or wrong, but it does matter that both failed to build trust, resulting in disaster. My sin was not forgiving Bill, who I thought was a betrayer; however, I found that forgiveness at his funeral when I heard words of praise for his recent life from loved ones and his pastor. He had rediscovered the peace of our Lord, and I was reminded of Jesus's parable in Matthew 20 of the workers in the vineyard. We all seem to worry too much about what we do in life compared to others. We have this sinful pride in our works and want to be elevated in the eyes of ourselves, others, and God for the amount of good works we do. Jesus tells us otherwise, saying that we should not compare and judge other people's worth and time of faithfulness but be satisfied in our own walk and relationship with God. God in his grace will reward each of us according to how he sees fit. It is not our place to take on God's role.

Judas betrayed Jesus for what seemed to be selfishness and thirty pieces of silver, but he really betrayed him because he lacked faith. He lost faith in Jesus because his didn't try to build trust by understanding Christ's real mission. Judas wanted to be elevated in the eyes of the leaders because he lost faith in Jesus.

When each of us fails to trust God, we are betraying him, just as Judas did. We are like the disciples who failed to stand up for Jesus in the days after Judas turned him over to the Jewish leaders. When we avoid using our talents for Christ, we are in essence denying knowing him, just as Peter denied knowing him. When we fail to continue building on our trust and faith, we are in denial of his greatness and complete power.

In our daily Christian walk, we should be about raising others up instead of trying to puff ourselves up before the world. We can fake humility, or we can seek the real thing by being faithful and trusting the real love of Christ. We should be joyful that Jesus will reward all who worked in his vineyard, no matter how long.

What you say and what you don't say are both important. To use proper speech, you must not only say the right words at the right time, you must also not say what you shouldn't. Examples of untamed tongue include gossiping, putting others down, bragging, manipulating, false teaching, exaggerating, complaining, flattering, and lying. Before you speak, ask, is what I want to say true? Is it necessary? Is it kind?

"Dear brothers and sisters, not many of you should become teachers in the church for we who teach will be judged by God with greater strictness.

"We all make many mistakes but those who control their tongues can also control themselves in every other way. We can make a large horse turn around and go wherever we want by means of a small bit in its mouth. And a tiny rudder makes a huge ship turn wherever the pilot wants it to go, even though the winds are strong. So also the tongue is a small thing, but what enormous damage it can do. A tiny spark can set a great forest on fire. And the tongue is a flame of fire. It is full of wickedness that can ruin your whole life. It can turn the entire course of your life into a blazing flame of destruction for it is set on fire by hell itself" (James 3:1–6).

"If you are wise and understand God's ways, live a life of steady goodness so that only good deeds will pour forth. And if you don't brag about the good you do, then you will be truly wise! But if you are bitterly jealous and there is selfish ambition in your hearts, don't brag about being wise. That is the worst kind of lie. For jealousy and selfishness are not God's kind of wisdom. Such things are earthly, unspiritual, and motivated by the devil. For wherever there is jealousy and selfish ambition, there you will find disorder and every kind of evil. But the wisdom that comes from heaven is first of all pure. It is also peace loving, gentle at all times, and willing to yield to others. It is full of mercy and good deeds. It shows no partiality and is always sincere. And those who are peacemakers will plant seeds of peace and reap a harvest of goodness" (James 3:13–18).

1. Have you ever failed to use your tongue to praise Jesus when the opportunity arose?
2. Have you spread gossip?
3. Have you ever failed to speak up for someone being harmed by gossip?
4. Do you sometimes feel you are doing more than your share of work in the church?
5. Do you ever brag about your good deeds and charitableness?
6. Do you have trouble forgiving others?

Boxes

Question: What was the most interesting box you ever opened? Did it contain something of value, like a letter or jewelry or your mother's Bible?

I once opened a box, a gift from my mother, which held a gold watch. It was my dad's watch. To this day, it is the only thing I have that was his. When I wear it, I think of all the Christian values he represented.

I have often thought of the fact that we all live in a box of sorts, and we get into another box to drive to work. We keep our stuff in locked boxes and keep our food in a big cold box. We give gifts in boxes. Boxes are ubiquitous in our lives.

We create storage boxes for our minds when thoughts and memories become too troublesome. We store these away, opening them occasionally as respite for refreshment from new life experiences. I have learned that if I open these old boxes from time to time, I can find things that can be damaging to living a good life, now and into the future. Old prejudices may be feeding the now without the cleansing effects of better information. We may lack some trust, which is necessary for the love taught by our Christian faith. We drag old boxes from under the bed or closets to see if the contents have value and discard them if they no longer are useful, so why don't we do the same with our mental or spiritual storage boxes?

Last week in a discussion with my wife, I said that some people do not want to be active Christians. Some just want to be lukewarm Christians. Mary disagreed, saying that she thought most want to be good Christians but may be too shy or maybe lazy. She was right to a degree; however, I still believe that sometimes, we just want to put our faith in a box and hide it under the bed.

We are having political disagreements over the inclusion of faith and religion in public institutions. We are currently having disagreements over whether it's appropriate to stand for our national anthem. There is an element of faith in God associated with this flag ceremony ("One nation under God"). A sub context of unity and love of God each other and country is implied to most Americans. We are told we need to separate our faith from many aspects of our lives. We are to put this faith in a box and store it until Sunday, so to speak. I think this becomes too easy to do. It becomes comfortable for us to separate our faith from most aspects of living.

If you believe in a creator of all things visible and invisible, then as a Christian, you must believe that this creator cares if we have feelings of love. There should be a correlating belief, given the aforementioned belief that this power permeates all things. This energy source we Christians refer to as God permeates all things in our lives. If God is present in all things, then as Christians, we should not try to eliminate or hide his presence from anything or anybody. We should present our faith and the values it represents in every action, thought, and activity. We should not separate it from political ideas, civic duties, or our work or profession. If the God we Christians venerate exists, then we should promote this loving deity in who we are. If this loving God offends others, then so be it. Our God does not like being stored in a box under our bed. True Christian love softens our message, making it easier to disseminate without rancor. Who can get offended by true love? How is it possible as a Christian to separate this faith from our business or profession? How is it possible to keep it from our schools or civic institutions?

Jesus was who he said he was, or else he was totally insane, and all his disciples were insane to follow him, even to their martyrdom. I doubt that even lukewarm Christians think Jesus was crazy, so it makes you wonder why they would want to keep their Christianity hidden in a box. Christianity is either of little importance or the most important movement this universe has ever known. If Christianity is of the utmost importance, then we should be promoting it in every aspect of our lives. We should not be anything less than full-amperage Christians.

"Love is patient and kind. Love is not jealous or boastful or proud or rude. Love does not demand its own way. Love is not irritable and it keeps no record of when it has been wronged. It is never glad about injustice but rejoices whenever the truth wins out. Love never gives up, never loses faith, is always hopeful, and endures through every circumstance" (1 Corinthians 13:4). (Substitute the word *Christianity* for *love* to better understand.)

1. Have you ever heard someone say, "God and I have our own thing going," meaning "I don't need a church"?
2. What aspect of your life do you exclude God?
3. Do you believe if we try to eliminate God from our institutions, we are virtuous in his eyes?
4. Have you ever failed to stand up for God?
5. Why not call upon that source of strength and wisdom to be a better Christian?
6. Do you have any boxes under a bed or in a closet in your mind or soul that need airing out?
7. Is your Bible at the top of the stack of books at your chairside? Where is it?

"Christianity, if false, is of no importance, and if true, of infinite importance. The only thing it cannot be is moderately important."—C. S. Lewis

While you were busy judging others, you left your box open and your skeletons fell out.

Lord, I have kept you hidden all these many years.
I have suffered and shed so many lonely tears.

If only I would have opened that door to you in my inner being,
my lonely walk through life would have had much more meaning.

The pain I suffered thinking I was alone through it all,
This lesson is often learned too late to prevent a fall.

Now knowing joy and love as I hold your offered hand,
It is my strength and comfort as I travel toward a Promised Land.

Changes in Attitudes

Question: Do you believe politics should be avoided in all Christian commentary and discussions? Contrarily, has it become impossible to unravel moral issues and politics?

Harper Lee, the author of *To Kill a Mockingbird,* a book that sold millions in the early sixties, wrote another novel earlier that was not published until recently. The manuscript was discovered in her bank lock box, where it had been ignored for years. The book generated some controversies because the saintly Atticus appears to have been a segregationist in the first novel. Some think this subtracts from his character, who defended Tom on the false rape charges in an atmosphere of racism in their town in the award-winning book. Others suggest Atticus should be judged as a man in his time and place.

Politicians are often accused of flip-flopping on issues and are condemned for having one opinion in the past and changing their position. This raises the question, is it wrong to change your mind? If this is so, I am afraid we are all guilty. We've all changed our minds when new information became available or we become better informed. Just as Scout and her older brother changed their attitude about Boo Radley when they got to know him after he saved Jem's life. We all at times change our feelings about people when we really get to know them. There have been times when I thought I didn't care for someone, only to discover they were very different when I got to know them better. I can think of political issues that I was certain I was on the right side, only to find years later, I was on the wrong side. I hated all Japanese during the war but found after the war ended that they weren't all cruel and evil. I understand, however, that their regime had to be defeated militarily for the good people to emerge. Many believe that radical Islam ideology will have to be defeated militarily in a similar manner. Others say we should be careful not to offend good Muslims and try to reason with them. Perhaps we should have reasoned more with Hitler and been more careful not to offend the German people.

My grandfather was once a member of the Ku Klux Klan because he thought his values were being challenged by members of other races and other religions. He was not an evil man but captured in a different time and place. His ideology was slowly defeated, culturally and politically; however, it took years for most of us to change our attitude, while a few remain misguided, even to this day.

My grandfather changed over the years, and hopefully, we all change for the better as we grow older. It is an unfortunate fact that some of us change for the worse because we hear information that is incomplete or distorted or seek information from limited sources. There are some among us who will change with any blowing wind, not developing values that ground their thoughts and actions. Some become closed-minded and intransigent to the point that they seldom let any new information affect their opinions; they consider their values to be set in stone.

There is one source we can always go to for guidance, which is our God. Jesus never rushed to get the opinion of others. He wanted to know only what God thought. Before he called the twelve apostles to service, Jesus spent an entire night praying alone (Luke 6:12). Jesus then waited for God to give him guidance. We all can find blessings in solitude with God, if we listen for his answer with our whole being. We sometimes have to suffer, just as our Lord Jesus suffered, in order to better understand love.

There was a time when I didn't believe that suffering was a gift; instead, I thought it was a curse. I remember the night I spent with my dad, who was in a hospital with two types of cancer. It happened to be the night before his wedding anniversary. He was in great pain. In the middle of the night, I went to his bed, fluffed his pillow, and rubbed his back.

In a mental fog, he asked me why he had to suffer like this in order to get married the next day. "Did you have to suffer like this, Jimmy, before you got married?"

"No, Dad," I responded. "I didn't."

As I tried to comfort him in his last hours, I prayed for God to help him. I don't guess I listened to God's answer at the time. I have since understood that the suffering we are blessed with brings us closer to the comforting arms of Jesus. In Gethsemane, Jesus prayed for relief from his suffering, but in the end, he accepted his pain as the ultimate way to love God. Suffering often precedes something good. My father somehow understood this, as he related his suffering to a requirement before a blessing. I could have cursed my God that night for taking my dad, but I have since learned more about God's love and changed my attitude. Our attitude can be changed by listening closer to our Lord.

Just like Atticus, who was once a segregationist, I was taught to think that way in my youth. Since my misinformed youth, I have changed my attitude and understand that I was wrong. I also understand how I was misinformed. My parents brought the misinformation they had been taught, because of ignorance, to my brother and me.

The culture was making fumbling attempts to change for the good in Atticus Finch's fictional time, as in my grandfather's real time. We should each ask ourselves if the cultural changes we are witnessing are from bad to good or from good to bad. Should we be so strident in our loyalty to a political party that we stand by as politics becomes corrupted to the point of leading us away from our God?

There have been attempts recently to change certain values. Science tells us that babies born with two X chromosomes are female, and those born with X and Y chromosomes are male. If they decide to change their orientation, we are told we should accept them to be whatever they say they are. If a man says he is a woman, then we are to accept him as a woman. Reality informs us he will still have the X and Y chromosome configuration in every cell of his body and will still be a male, no matter what he says.

The sacrament of marriage was created for a man and woman to become committed in the sight of God and humankind to a life together for the purpose of propagating life on earth. Now some people ask us to change the meaning of matrimony because of a fundamental right, so a union between the same sex will be recognized by our Christian church.

I think we are to be tolerant of other people and understand their desires for a loving relationship. However, we should not change the meaning of words and institutions in order to soothe the sensibilities of anyone who wants approval of their lifestyle. We should let God sort out things that we cannot figure out.

Political controversies have resulted in the breakup of many churches and even relationships of church members. We have become so polarized by politicians that we avoid discussing important issues for the continuation of our Christian churches. People sometimes move to another church because they have difficulty accepting decisions made by church leaders. Isn't it time for all Christians to take a stand on certain moral issues, even sensitive ones? We are so careful not to offend anyone that we stand by as our long-held beliefs are destroyed or ridiculed, to the point of being afraid to speak up. As Christians, should we seek a monastic type of life or speak up to defend our traditional values?

Take gay marriage, one issue confronting us today. Why can't we discuss it without rancor or division? One side says everyone should be able to marry whoever they love. The other side says our Christian tradition says marriage is a union between a man and a woman. Some want the blessings of the church on unions between two men or women, with the marriage being performed by our clergy. Our scriptures are pretty clear that homosexual acts are sinful. Jesus addressed this in Mathew 19:4–5. Paul was clear in 1 Corinthians 6:9–10 that homosexual acts are sinful. Should we change our scripture? If we are asked to go along with this, what is next? Some people want to be able to have relations with children, so will we be asked sometime in the future to accept this behavior? Some men desire multiple wives; will we be asked to denigrate women to accommodate these men? Are we to give up moral positions about sexual behavior because some of us want our desires to have an official stamp of approval? People are still allowed most any behavior they want to follow, but we should not be required to agree, as long as they do not attempt to change black into white and demand approval.

Another issue that has become extremely political is abortion. One side says that the fetus is a life, a baby that needs to be protected. The other side says it should be the choice of the mother; it is her body. We now learn that certain groups are advocating the use of body parts from babies that have been aborted. A lab worker recently stated that she had no sense of wrongness about her job of sorting through the aborted tissue until she picked up a little arm with her tweezers. What had been fetal tissue suddenly became a human. Physicians have presented strong views in our Bible study group, saying that we should not interfere with a woman's choice because the resulting birth could cause stress. If they had to sort through the aborted tissue, they might change their attitude.

Nature is unfair at times and imperfect in some eyes, but this does not authorize us to attempt to change nature. We are living in an imperfect world; we need to learn to love God. We should not let our love of ourselves become our God. We sometimes take wrong positions and learn the truth over time; with information and discussion and knowledge, we learn why we were wrong. Other times we were right and should have defended our position more strongly. We should be open to other well-meaning individuals as sources of information, as long as it does not change our love of God and other people.

We sometimes think we can change the essence of something just by changing the name. Relief became welfare, which then became family service, but it is still the government taking money from someone to help someone else. An unborn baby has become a fetus. Abortion becomes family planning, but in many people's minds, it is still ending a life.

We can call a sunrise a sunset if we want to, but the sun will still be coming up in the east.

"Now let's talk about food that has been sacrificed to idols. You think that everyone should agree with your perfect knowledge. While knowledge may make us feel important, it is love that really builds up the Church. Anyone who claims to know all the answers doesn't really know very much. But the person who loves God is the one God knows and cares for" (1 Corinthians 8:1–3).

"Don't you know that those who do wrong, will have no share in the Kingdom of God? Don't fool yourselves. Those who indulge in sexual sin, who are idol worshipers, adulterers, male prostitutes, homosexuals, thieves, greedy people, drunkards, abusers, and swindlers—none of these will have a share in the Kingdom of God" (1 Corinthians 6:9–10).

1. If our culture had not changed its attitude about sexual sins, would there not be a lot of us stoned to death?
2. It seems that sometimes opinions become idols, and we are all asked to worship someone else's idol. Does this sound familiar in our culture today?
3. Should sinners be encouraged to attend our church but not ask us to worship their idols? Are we not all sinners?
4. In Leviticus 20:10, it says, "If a man commits adultery with another man's wife both the man and the woman must be put to death." We seem to have changed our attitude about this punishment, have we not?
5. In Leviticus 20:13, the penalty for homosexual acts is death to both parties. Should we still do this?
6. What is the difference between tolerance and approval? Did Jesus ask for certain scriptures to be changed or for people to change their attitude?
7. Should we change our church affiliation if we disagree with changes or stay and fight?
8. If science proves that homosexuality has a genetic component, will that change your attitude? If you have a child or grandchild who is gay, will you have a more understanding attitude?
9. We now know that alcoholism has a genetic component, but it can be controlled by those afflicted; is the same perhaps true of homosexuality?

Christian Churches

Question: Do you believe everything your church teaches and stands for? Can you still belong to a church that promotes something you don't completely agree with?

There are deep emotional divisions not only among the many Christian denominations but even within each denomination. The worldview of the hierarchy of some churches is not held by all the members. We have differences within all churches about so-called social issues: abortion, birth control, homosexuality, women's roles, sex outside of marriage, government's role in supporting people, divorce, and same-sex marriage, to name a few. Everyone reading this will have different views on these issues. The question arises, should we seek a church that fits all of our ideals perfectly? If we cannot find such a church, should we just have our own church? What is a church? Does a church exist that you agree with all their espoused principles, dogma, and mode of worship?

We often agree to laws passed by our governing bodies, but after rule making and implementation, we discover unintentional effects that cause us to question our original consent. Many laws are passed by our government that sounded wonderful in their original intent but turn out to be disastrous after implementation. Governing bodies of Christian denominations are by the same human frailty subject to misunderstanding and even misinterpretation of scriptures and social solutions. The Roman Catholic Church is aware of this therefore very slow to make changes, often to the dismay of members who seek changes to fit their vision of faith. Methodists disagree with the concept of papal infallibility when speaking ex cathedra about faith and dogma. Methodists believe the only legitimate head of the Christian church is the Lord Jesus Christ. Today, there are even some within the Catholic faith who question the pope's power and authority, even though Catholic doctrine teaches it was bestowed upon Peter by Jesus and continuous through all popes.

We should ask ourselves if we believe any church leader or leadership is infallible. If we do think church leaders can make mistakes in designing and implementing doctrine or interpreting scriptures, should we seek another church? By what criteria?

I had a friend who thought his minister was preaching anti-Semitism one Sunday; because of this, he quit going to any church. I have friends who disagreed with other ministers' sermons and management decisions, which caused them to move to other churches or quit going to any church. Sometimes, church members feel their church work or ministry is unappreciated and therefore quit their church. All of us have known people who thought their gifts to the church were ignored or misused.

Are we to quit any church that does not fit our matrix of Christianity? Are we to oppose anyone seeking God and offering their service by talents valuable to Christ's mission because we think they are sinning, according to our scriptural understanding? If we do apply this standard for church membership and leadership, there will be no one left to throw stones or build stone works. If we don't find our minister to be inspiring enough, should we replace him or find a more dynamic speaker at another church?

I personally believe that when we seek a relationship with God, we should keep our focus upon him and the teachings of his Son, Jesus, which is to love our God with all our heart and all our soul, and to love one another as we love ourselves. If we continue to do this, we will walk away from the stoning of others because we are busy trying to improve our own Christian lives. We will continue to sin because we are human, just as our church leaders will make mistakes because they are human. Must we think the early church leaders were infallible? Were the bishops who declared certain scriptures to be the ones included in our Bible infallible? If so, why were changes made over the centuries? Certain concepts are becoming less acceptable by Christians and seem unreasonable by today's standards, while some apostles wrote as if they had the imprimatur of Jesus, even though he was silent on those issues, such as women being silent in church and being subservient to their husbands (1 Corinthians 14:34). You may argue that was because of the Corinthian culture. Was then Paul's statement that homosexuals who acted on their sexuality were sinners only true for that culture? If we quietly go to others to inform them of their sins, I am afraid they may point out a few of our own. How would it work if we just had one big stone-throwing service a year and pointed out each other's sins?

"Then Jesus told this story to some who had great self-confidence and scorned everyone else: Two men went to the Temple to pray. One was a Pharisee, and the other was a dishonest tax collector. The proud Pharisee stood by himself and prayed this prayer: I thank you, God, that I am not a sinner like everyone else, especially like that tax collector over there! For I never cheat, I don't sin, I don't commit adultery. I fast twice a week and I give you a tenth of my income.

"But the tax collector stood at a distance and dared not even lift his eyes to heaven as he prayed. Instead, he beat his chest in sorrow, saying. O God, be merciful to me, for I am a sinner. I tell you, this sinner, not the Pharisee returned home justified before God. For the proud will be humbled, but the humble will be honored" (Luke 18:9–14).

Abraham was, humanly speaking, the founder of our Jewish nation. What were his experiences concerning this question of being saved by faith? Was it because of his good deeds that God accepted him? If so, he would have had something to boast about. But from God's point of view, Abraham had no basis at all for pride.

For the scriptures tell us, "Abraham believed God, so God declared him to be righteous.

"Then people work, their wages are not a gift. Workers earn what they receive. But people are declared righteous because of their faith, not because of their work.

"King David spoke of this, describing the happiness of an undeserving sinner who is declared to be righteous:

"'Oh, what joy for those whose disobedience is forgiven.

"'Whose sins are put out of sight.

"'Yes, what joy for those

"'Whose sin is no longer counted against them by the Lord?'" (Romans 4:1–8).

1. If we don't allow church membership or leadership to people we consider to be sinners, should we by the same reason give up our own roles?
2. Jesus usually taught us to avoid judgment, but is it sometimes necessary to make judgments?
3. I didn't agree with our Methodist hierarchy when they made statements about our Cuban relationship. Should I have found another church?
4. Should you find another church if you don't like a preacher?
5. If you don't agree with something about your church, do you take the time to discuss it with the pastor?
6. Do you think of your church as "the pastor, the building, the brothers and sisters in the fold"?

A man can make mistakes but he is not a failure until he starts blaming others.

Christianity by the Cafeteria Plan

Question: Do you believe the Bible is the inspired word of God and we as Christians are required to believe everything in it?

We who claim to be Christians quite often want to pick and choose what parts of our scriptures to follow. Not many of us would want to give up our wealth, much less our very life, to follow Christ. There have been many during the two thousand years of Christianity who have given their all to serve Christ as examples of human love, endeavor, and discipline. God does not ask us to give up living; however, he does ask us to love and provide self-discipline in following Christ. We are asked to offer our all in the love of Christ in order to receive the Holy Spirit.

Trappist monks and nuns take vows of obedience, poverty, and chastity, in order to become more Christ like. They do not take vows of silence, as is popularly believed; however, they do refrain from speaking as much as possible in order to be more contemplative in their lifestyle. The Trappists are a subset of the Cistercians, who follow the Benedictine example; their order was founded in 1098.

In our contemporary world, we often laugh at people and call them extremists if they give up the enjoyment of worldly things and practices. To give up sex in today's secular world is thought of as ridiculous. Why would anyone give up these basic urges in order to express their love for Christ? It would be asking too much for nothing in return. Why would anyone give up wealth and live in poverty to serve some antiquated religious devotion?

I would wager that most of us would give up anything in order to serve and glorify Christ if we knew he was returning to this world in a few weeks. Well, he did inform us that he was going to return; speaking of wagers, consider Pascal's Wager. If you wager that there is no God and win, you win nothing and risk everything; if you wager there is a God and win, you win everything while risking nothing. Why not make the second option a way of life and begin serving Christ? You have nothing to lose and everything to gain.

The politically correct denizens of the secular world are trying to coerce any Christian zeal to be seen as extremist, even to the point of removing Christ from Christmas. To believe Christ is the Son of God would be ridiculous in this informed and tolerant world, so to avoid being ridiculed, why not just become lukewarm Christians? To sacrifice as a sign of love for Christ is foolish; we should never be condemned for any kind of sexual pleasure we seek. We should be allowed to follow whatever deranged behavior we desire, as long as it is consensual. The sin of adultery is passé in a tolerant world. Same-sex marriage should be accommodated or even venerated. To love everyone in agape love is laughable.

Here are some things chosen from the table at the Christian cafeteria by a lukewarm Christian:

1. Go to church often, if convenient.
2. Give some to the church, if it does not restrict your lifestyle.
3. Be on the popular side, but don't stand up against the popular beliefs, which may be wrong.
4. Want to be saved from the penalty of sin, not from sin itself.
5. Avoid condemning sin.
6. See sin as relative, with many gray areas.
7. Imagine Jesus would be tolerant of most any sin because he understands.
8. Never share Christianity because it may offend someone.
9. Don't believe Romans 1:26–27 or 1 Timothy 1:10 are acceptable in today's informed world.

"Because you are like lukewarm water, neither hot nor cold, I will spit you out of my mouth" (Revelation 3:16).

1. Are you willing to go with the unpopular side in order to honor Christ?
2. Do you just want to go to church and live your life without anyone telling you what is right?
3. Have you ever stayed quiet when you should have stood up for your Christian belief?
4. When was the last time you sacrificed anything for your Christian faith?

Our devotion to Christianity often melts in the strong solvent of political correctness, allowing us to appear to have Christ like tolerance.

Death

Question: Do you feel anxious about dying? Do you fear death or look forward to it?

I guess I have a certain amount of anxiety about my last breath. I pray that God's mercy is as great as my need for it. I think I would like to die laughing, with friends and relatives laughing with me. I want to do it right because I can only do it once.

I have been with a few friends and relatives and even a few strangers when they moved from this life to the next. I don't think of any of them showed fear. There was a tranquility about them and maybe somewhat of a detachment from a consciousness of this life. I engaged some in conversation; they focused on my questions for a moment but usually seemed to be elsewhere. My grandmother was alone in a hospital room when I went to visit her on her last day. I sat beside her and tried to get her to talk, but she just stared at the ceiling. I finally thought of a story she always told about me as a child that she thought was terribly funny. When I repeated the story as she had told it so many times, she looked at me for a second and chuckled softly. I felt that she was waiting to be escorted to the next life, but the familiar story made her look back for a second.

When my father was dying, he showed no fear but asked the question, "Am I dying?" Trusting in a medical knowledge he thought his son had may have been excessive, but he seemed satisfied when I told him no. I told him that the doctor had given him some medicine that made him feel strange. He said okay but then shortly after, he died.

I know that many people die horrible deaths with fear, pain, and suffering. I know somehow our loving God will take that into consideration when he fits them in their heavenly robe. The same holds true for those who don't live a long life. We are all one step from death at any time during our time here; it may be a roll of the dice, or it may be part of God's mysterious plan. I believe that we should live each day with that in the back of our mortal mind as we go about our tasks. We all should attempt to live a life for the love Christ died for.

I've been with some close friends on their last few hours or days; they've just given me a smile and a squeezed my hand to show their confidence in the trip they were embarking upon. I believe that those who had an illness or were advanced in age were lucky. They had a chance to say their prayers and tell family and friends goodbye. On some occasions, death comes suddenly, by accident or by the failure of a vital organ. In those cases, there is not time to say goodbye or ask for forgiveness. I pray that in those cases, our Lord understands their state of love for him, and forgiveness is given without words spoken. We seem unable to define the exact moment of death; the person dying is moving into a realm where time is irrelevant. Many people think if you have not uttered the words of supplication and forgiveness before the heart stops, you have waited too long. I guess I will leave the truth to those who have a better connection than me.

Unfortunately, over the years, our churches have acted a little like the Pharisees in Jesus's time. There have been so many requirements placed between our soul's relationships with God, it's confusing. I suppose that is why we have so many different Christian denominations. Here again, I will have to leave that up to each individual and their God. It seems to me that Jesus mentioned and showed tolerance when he walked this earth. He also disliked a lot of ceremony and frivolous rules.

Some people want to be remembered after they are gone by having buildings and highways or colleges named after them. Some want great gravestones that will somehow make people think they were important. Then there are the rest of us, who just pray that our life had some meaning and perhaps we made a small contribution. I read a quote recently by Shannon Alder: "Carve your name on hearts, not tombstones. A legacy is etched into the minds of others and the stories they share about you." I suppose this is my philosophy. I have always wanted to live a life of love, improving each day, and by that love leave someone's life better for the love I left with them. We can live on in our children and friends by leaving the example of a life well lived. We should not fear death any more than the sleep brought on by a well-lived day. We have been sent the Son of God to light the way and take away death's sting.

"Nevertheless, that time of darkness and despair will not go on forever. The land of Zebulun and Naphtali will soon be humbled, but there will be a time in the future when Galilee of the Gentiles, which lies along the road that runs between the Jordan and the sea, will be filled with glory. The people who walk in darkness will see a great light—a light that will shine on all who live in the land where death casts its shadow" (Isaiah 9:1–2).

1. Is it better to ignore death and live as if we will live in this world forever?
2. Would you rather be leaving on a trip and waving goodbye to loved ones or staying behind while they leave?
3. For those who think we have to utilize certain rituals such as baptism, was not Jesus's giving the thief on the cross eternal life something to dispute rituals?
4. What is a good age to die?
5. What will your last words be? Why are you not thinking of them now?
6. Will we be absolved of sins we forgot to ask forgiveness for?

"Life is stronger than death even though it can't stop death from happening, but no matter how hard death tries it can't separate people from love. It can't take away our memories either. In the end, life is stronger than death."—Unknown

"Cancer sometimes gets a bad rap. At least it gives one a chance to say goodbye."—Dr. John Christy

"I can't think of a more wonderful thanksgiving for the life I have had than that everyone should be jolly at my funeral."—Lord Mountbatten

"You gotta keep laughing."—Dr. A. D. Brookreson

"It is said, your life flashes before your eyes just before dying. That is true, it's called life." Terry Pratchett, *The Last Continent*

"By God, Woodrow; it's been quite a party."—Gus McCrae, *Lonesome Dove*

"Well, adios, boys; hope you won't hold it against me. I never meant no harm."—Jake Spoon, *Lonesome Dove*

Disagreement

Question: What is something about which there is disagreement causing conflict, that you deem important to develop agreement?

Since the beginning of human consciousness, there have been disagreements. Our Bible tells us this is a fact as well as our empirical knowledge. It is my belief that these disruptions of human relationships and experiences are transcendental, having as a source the wisdom of God to allow humans to seek understanding of love.

Each human has a mind that utilizes a brain. Some brains are better constructed and allow greater platforms for the mind to function than others. The pursuit of love requires the greater minds to develop and utilize ways to give lessor minds pathways to understanding that they would otherwise not be capable of. We Christians should agree upon this basic concept. We humans utilize our actions and reactions to inform others. Language developed so that better understanding of concepts and events could result. Different languages evolved, utilizing different sounds and inflections. Some languages appear to be more functional on certain discourses than others. The so-called dead language of Latin is often utilized as a safe haven for deep thoughts. We also have developed an understanding of physics, mathematics, music, and other art forms to communicate ideas and emotions. We have our five basic senses to accumulate information in our minds; using our brains, we analyze this information and react to it.

In the process of human intercourse, all humans arrive with different experiences and different minds, which can cause conflict. In order for social development to happen, it becomes necessary for minds coming from different experiences and inputs to find areas of agreement. These agreements should always be guided by our ultimate goal of understanding love. It is a fact that words, languages, are poor bridges whereby thoughts are transferred from one mind to another. When emotions are misinformed, this transfer can be difficult. When words are called upon by one individual to inform another individual, there are emotions involved in the process by both individuals. These emotions, along with the limitations of ignorance of some degree, may allow improper words and poor sentence structures to present concepts ineffectively. To say this in a more mundane way, we don't always say what we mean, and we don't always hear what was said.

Sometimes, our lack of information and understanding does not allow minds to meet and agree. When this happens, we should go back to our ultimate goal of understanding love as the most important emotional processing element. Love often if not always requires efforts to understand how the opposing mind developed. This is called empathy. The old Native American adage comes to mind: "If you have not walked a mile in the other man's moccasins, you will not understand him."(If you still are in disagreement you will at least be a mile away from him and have his shoes!)

Often political disagreements are not philosophically far apart, but the disagreement is over the solution. Even when a solution is agreed on, laws are often passed that are poorly implemented. The language used to describe a law is often unclear.

In order to resolve conflict, we need to examine both our own emotional barriers and the emotional barriers of others. This is the beginning of achieving our ultimate goal: understanding, living, and spreading the gift of God's love.

Our Lord Jesus used simple words to describe the ultimate:

"Then Jesus told him, 'I have come to judge the world. I have come to give sight to the blind and to show those who think they see that they are blind'" (John 9:39).

"Language is the dress of thought."—Samuel Johnson

Conflict results from the misuse of language.

1. Do you often let anger choose your words for you?
2. During a conflict, do you let the other person's anger infect your response?
3. How do you avoid emotional interference in relationships?
4. Where do you think the bricks of your emotional wall came from?
5. Do you sometimes fail to utilize an apology to buy time to resolve a misunderstanding?
6. Are the differences in religions only differences in understanding love from different perspectives, due to life experiences?
7. Are conflicts between Democrats and Republicans because of different perspectives, due to life experiences?
8. Are conflicts between husbands and wives because of different perspectives, due to life experiences?

Kantian philosophy would describe *transcendental* as relating to an experience as determined by the mind's makeup. Love results when we utilize our five senses to enjoy our world in a similar fashion.

Don't Worry; Be Happy

Question: What do you worry about the most?

When my wife was diagnosed with an aggressive type of breast cancer not long ago. In the process of digesting this information, she told me that one of her main concerns is that knowing herself to be a worrier, she will worry about all aspects of this for the remainder of her life. We have both prayed for enlightenment from God while we process this challenge. God gave me something in my spirit that night that I was to share with Mary. I knew that I was to tell her to be alert to God speaking to her over the next couple days. I asked her if she thought of me as a sincere person who spoke from my heart about God and our relationship with him. She looked at me with amazement that I would ask her something that was a given to her.

"Why, sure," she said. "Why do you ask?"

I told her that God was going to speak to her in some way in the next couple days, and she would know it when it happened, so stay alert to God's voice. The next morning, she told me that in the middle of the night, she awoke, worrying as she often does, when she heard a strong wind blowing outside, bringing her some kind of peace. As she was telling me this, she was looking at something on her I-Pad. I asked what she was looking at, and she said they were asked in her Bible study for their favorite verse, and hers jumped at her from a couple sources this morning. She said that she thought this was the message God meant for her to hear. She also thought the wind of calmness was part of her message. I felt chills as I listened to her and felt God's presence with us, a presence that is always there if we are aware of it. After she left the room, I picked up a Bible and tried to remember the verse she mentioned. As I opened the Bible, it fell open, and I read a passage on the right page, thinking, *this doesn't mean much to me this morning.* Then I looked to the left-hand page, and there was the very verse that she had referred to, only a few moments before. As I read the passage, I remembered a conversation with a dear friend suffering from lung cancer. He told me he had discovered that he had more faith than he thought when he was faced with his diagnosis and treatment. My friend asked me to tell Mary to begin each day with a prayer of thanksgiving and faith that God will shoulder our worries if we allow him.

Just as I was writing this, I received a text from my daughter Dawne; she reassured me that God was working through us, and this is not my mind playing tricks on me. The following is that text:

Small Straws in a Soft Wind, by Marsha Burns

"Be quiet. It is in your best interest to stop worrying and fretting and start putting your trust in Me. For I will show you the way and be with you on this journey. Be sensitive to My leading and do not rely on your own thoughts and desires. I know what is best for you says the Lord. Have faith!"

"But let all those rejoice who put their trust in You; Let them ever shout for joy, because you defend them; Let those also who love Your name be joyful in You. For You, O Lord, will bless the righteous; with favor You will surround him as with a shield" (Psalm 5:11–12).

Dawne did not know what Mary and I were struggling with, but God worked through her to get an important message to all of us that morning. The Bible verse that Mary found so strong was from Philippians 4:6:

"Don't worry about anything; instead, pray about everything. Tell God what you need, and thank him for all he has done. If you do this, you will experience God's peace, which is far more wonderful than the human mind can understand. His peace will guard your hearts and minds as you live in Christ Jesus."

My God has restored my vision, which was being devastated by macular degeneration. A few months ago, my doctor said I was going from the "dry kind" to the "wet kind" and showed me the photos of my macula, indicating disruption behind my retina. He said that it was like bubbles, and they would soon break, leaving me with a hole in my vision. I left his office that day and prayed to accept my fate; it was also a prayer of faith.

On the next visit, the doctor showed me the new photo, saying that all the disturbance on my last visit was gone. I praised the Lord and gave him the credit, asking for understanding of what I was to do with my newfound vision. I didn't think it was given so that I could play more golf, although I certainly could see the ball with clearness that had not been there for a couple years. I do believe that for some reason, God has chosen me and my sweet wife, Mary, to exalt him in ways that he will show us as we travel a path filled with light and faith. I will be quiet and listen to God as I put my trust in his total wisdom.

1. God will speak to all of those who listen. Do you quietly listen or are you busy giving God instructions?
2. A miracle is usually only believed if it happens to you. Even Jesus's disciples struggled to believe even when they witnessed miracles. Why do we want to avoid seeing that God continues to work through us?
3. Do you ever feel God wants you to pass something on to a friend or acquaintance in need, emotionally or spiritually?
4. Have you ever been so absorbed in living life that you failed to appreciate it?
5. Do you believe God will work through you if you only allow him? Are you afraid to trust in the Lord? What are you afraid of?

We can trust that God will always meet our needs.

Endings

Question: Was there an ending that held significance in your life?

The sun was shining and no wind, but the cold air stung as I skied down a long run at Deer Valley, Utah. I had skied many times in Utah, Colorado, and even Europe over the twenty years preceding this trip to Utah. I had even skied this run a year before. I was skiing just ahead of my old friend Jim and looked over my shoulder to make sure he was keeping up. I saw him smile as he jumped a mogul and made a quick turn, throwing sparkling powder into the sunshine. It had been a great week, and we continued on to the bottom to a sliding stop, throwing more snow into the cold air and accenting the end of the final run of the day. I didn't know it at the time, but it was also the last time I would ski with my friend. In fact, it would be the last time I would ski anywhere. Three years later, that friend died of cancer.

I remember another time something was ending that I didn't realize at the time. I was trying out a Cherokee Lance airplane that I was considering to purchase. I had sold a four-place Mooney Mark 21 and wanted a six-place single-engine plane. The flight had been enjoyable while the salesman who had ferried the plane from Kansas City rode in the copilot seat telling me all the features of the aircraft. I had put it through many maneuvers that afternoon, including power-on stalls and power-off stalls. I really liked that aircraft. I had a few words with the salesman and left with his business card and a promise to call soon. It turned out to be the last time I would pilot an aircraft, after about a thousand hours of flight time over thirty-five years.

As he walked out the door of my pharmacy, my friend Butch turned and yelled, "I'll see you at the party tomorrow night."

"You bet," I responded without much thought. Butch would die on his Harley the next afternoon.

Everything in this life has an ending built in. Some endings are happy, some tragic, some mundane. The sad thing is that endings too often happen without our awareness. Some endings would be noted and celebrated in some manner if we had forewarning. If I had known that day as I pulled out of my mom's driveway in 1983 that she would die of a heart attack a few weeks later, I would have at least jumped out and hugged her instead of giving a perfunctory wave. I would have postponed whatever event I thought I needed to attend and stayed with her for the next three weeks.

Life is uncertain and fragile, but we assume that the things we enjoy will go on forever; unfortunately, we think our friends and family will always be there. We should at least live accordingly.

I know it is unreasonable to think that we can always anticipate endings and give them the appropriate attention; we are just humans who are trying to get through life. We want to enjoy life as much as possible. We study, plan, and work in order to have a good lifestyle and provide for our family. We enjoy our activities and assume we will always be able to enjoy them. Life, unfortunately, often has other plans.

I was watching the news last night when O'Reilly interviewed the parents of Kate Steinle, who had been killed at thirty-three years old. He asked her father, who was just walking with her in San Francisco on a family vacation, what her last words were.

Mr. Steinle, fighting tears, finally responded, "She said, 'help me, Dad.'"

I was overwrought, thinking, *what if that was my daughter?* I cannot imagine the terrible anguish. I have thought death can come so suddenly to anyone, even someone just enjoying a day with family. Understanding that we all must die sometime, I wonder why some have to die so tragically and at a young age. I can only come up with one answer: I believe God put us here to learn to love each other and through that process love God. We are given this life and told to appreciate life and our loved ones. We are to live life to the fullest but be careful because it is a dangerous world filled with evil and pitfalls. We are not promised to be safe from all dangers, but we are promised God will give us the strength and love to endure pain and suffering. We must understand that pain and suffering can bring us closer to the understanding of God's love.

Let us love each other while we can and appreciate this fragile life given us. Anger and hatred take us away from love and away from God.

Jesus tells us that he protects us from eternal harm. While believers can expect to suffer on this earth. Satan cannot harm their souls or take away their eternal life with God.

"I give them eternal life, and they will never perish. No one will snatch them away from me. For my Father has given them to me, and he is more powerful than anyone else. So no one can take them from me. The Father and I are one" (John 10:28–30).

1. Is there anyone you love that you need to contact today?
2. Do you carry anger at someone or even God for taking something from you?
3. We all lose friends and relatives. Why do you feel singled out when you suffer a loss?
4. Do you think of death as something permanent or just the doorway to another life?
5. If you lost someone and believe they are with Jesus in heaven, why would you want to bring them back?
6. How can you turn a tragic death into something good?

Enlightenment

Question: What do you think is the most important thing for life to continue on earth?

I would guess that many would answer this question with "oxygen" or, perhaps, "water." Some will think of carbon, the main building block of living organisms. If we consider the development of something called life, in order to distinguish it from un-living things, we have to understand that living things have the ability to repair damage, while un-living things do not. These repairs require energy. The source of energy is the radiation from the sun: light.

It is my belief that Einstein's theory of relativity gives us the answer to how it all began. $E = MC^2$ is beyond my ability and comprehension; however, in the simplest terms, its energy equals mass times the speed of light squared. There is always an interchange between energy and mass. Time, which requires change, measures the process. God, being the source of all energy, said, "Let there be light," and there was light (the Big Bang) The author of the book of Genesis did not understand anything about chlorophyll or the pyrrole rings that surround a magnesium atom, which make up the chemical substance necessary to convert the energy from light (photosynthesis) into the plants necessary for animal life and ultimately human life. He didn't understand that human hemoglobin is very similar, except an iron atom replaces the magnesium. He did understand that the light from the sun was the first thing our Lord created and therefore must have been the most important thing for life on earth to develop. Those who do not believe that God created the heavens and the earth will go to all measures to find how it all happened, but they ultimately have to go to the fact that there had to be an original energy source. The necessity for time to begin was as a result of God converting his energy into mass, thus beginning time.

Jesus was sent to us by our God to enlighten the world. When you want there to be no mistake, you deliver a message yourself. This is what God did by becoming human; he brought his message directly to this world in his words through Jesus. After Jesus saved the woman from being stoned for adultery at the Mount of Olives, he told the people that he was "the light of the world" (John 8:12). He told us that if we followed him, we wouldn't be stumbling through the darkness, because we would have the light that leads to life. It is interesting that metaphors are often tied to laws of nature. If there was no truths in metaphors, they would have no meaning.

There is an old song made popular by Debbie Boone that comes to my mind. She may have been singing about a lover, but she could have been talking about Jesus when she sang a song written by Joseph Brooks titled "You Light up my Life"

"And you light up my life
You give me hope to carry on
You light up my days and fill my nights with song."

There are so many things going on in our world today that need enlightenment; there are forces that do not want light to be shined upon problems with true honesty because of political agendas. Christians often fear condemnation for speaking out. The political correctness and anti-religious forces do not want us to talk honestly about certain subjects because it will defeat them politically. Jesus did not let political correctness prevent him from telling the world it needed changing.

"How terrible it will be for you teachers of religious law and you Pharisees, Hypocrites! You are like whitewashed tombs—beautiful on the outside but filled on the inside with dead people's bones and all sorts of impurity. You try to look like upright people outwardly, but inside your hearts are filled with hypocrisy and lawlessness.

"How terrible it will be for you teachers of religious law and you Pharisees. Hypocrites! For you build tombs for the prophets your ancestors killed and decorate the graves of godly people your ancestors destroyed. Then you say, 'We never would have joined them in killing the prophets.'

"Snakes! Sons of vipers! How will you escape the judgment of hell?" (Matthew 23:27–33)

1. Are you afraid to speak your mind as a Christian because of political correctness?
2. When some Christian ideals are challenged, do you think we should try to understand where those who challenge them are coming from?
3. If we challenge the leadership roles held by gay people in our church, are we being strong in our faith or are we being Pharisees and hypocrites?
4. Abortion is a hot topic. Would you want more light on the subject, say filming the procedure and showing it to adults? How about public executions, like in some countries?
5. We want to be politically correct and not condemn Islam, but how about showing some of the punishments of their Sharia law?

"We need more light about each other; light creates understanding, understanding creates love, love creates patience, and patience creates unity."—Malcolm X

Fear

Question: What is something you fear?

There are many things to be fearful of in this world, like the dangerous things the foods we eat may contain, like hormones, pesticides, fat, and cholesterol. Drinking water is no longer safe, so we have to purchase our water in plastic bottles. Wait, there are chemicals in plastic that may leach into the water. We are even afraid of sunshine and the danger of skin cancer. We are afraid of evil in the world and avoid having children because we don't want them to be exposed to all this danger. We can become so fearful of this world God gave us; maybe we should never venture out into it, just stay in our home all day.

Well, there are also dangers in the home: radon gas may be under our house, spreading radiation all through our bodies. Some homes even have guns in them that may kill us or our children. Rodents bring in germs that might make us sick and die, so we are not even safe within the confines of our homes. What are we to do? We can't eat meat because we have to kill animals, and they may have hormones in their tissue. We can't wear leather because it takes an animal's life. We no longer are able to get a new automobile with leather interior because cows have feelings too. Try to get a 100 percent leather belt; they now are producing vegetable belts. I don't know what vegetables they use, but while shopping for a belt, I recently came across these new vegetable products (I guess we can eat them after we grow out of them).

The list of fearful things seems endless: atomic weapons, terrorists, acid rain, high places, small places, mercury, lead, germs, animal fat, alar on apples, lead paint, salt, artificial sweeteners, caffeine, perfumed colored toilet tissue, and how about the cranberry scare back in 1959? When I was a kid, my mom had me afraid of fish bones, ringworm, rabies, public toilet seats, polio, and Tomcat Palmer's son, Chalk-Eye Palmer. Many of us fear climate change will doom the whole world. The melting polar ice will raise the oceans and flood New York and Los Angeles. That might not be such a bad thing because that is where most of the people live who are making us fearful of the world.

Are we raising children to be afraid of the world? We are afraid to let them walk to school, ride bikes on the street, swim in the ocean, or play outside because of mosquitos carrying the Zika virus. We give them artificial milk and organic milk to avoid hormones in milk. I did see how one family dealt with the skin cancer problem; they all had long pants, long-sleeved shirts, floppy hats, and sunglasses when they played in the water. There were little children and elderly all covered from head to toe, splashing in the water. I wondered about the possible pollution they were exposed to and the dyes in their clothing that may cause cancer.

What has happened to common sense? We may not like the way God created our universe, but it is what we have, so why don't we live in it with the knowledge that our bodies were created to withstand much of the bacteria and contaminants we are exposed to? We need sunshine to convert 7-dehydrocholesterol in our skin to vitamin D. We need certain bacteria to live in our guts in a synergistic manner. Some people who are so fearful about the world believe this is all there is. They do not believe in God or an afterlife, so they want to live forever; therefore, anything that may be harmful should be avoided. Didn't David volunteer to fight Goliath because he was the only one not afraid to? David knew God would take care of him. Perhaps we should have the same faith today as we live our lives and bring children into our world. It feels so much safer knowing you have Jesus with you as you venture out into the world. We Christians profess to believe our scriptures, but we are sometimes hesitant to believe all of it. Were the animals not placed upon earth for our benefit? There have been five mass extinctions on earth, and the sixth one may come if we don't learn to love our God and each other.

"Suppose all these things happen to you—the blessings and the curses I have listed—and you mediate on them as you are living among the nations to which the Lord our God has exiled you. If at that time you return to the Lord your God, and you and your children begin wholeheartedly to obey all the commands I have given you today, then the Lord your God will restore your fortunes. He will have mercy on you and gather you back from all the nations where he has scattered you. Though you are at the ends of the earth, the Lord your God will go and find you and bring you back again. He will return you to the land that belonged to your ancestors, and you will possess that land again. He will make you even more prosperous and numerous than your ancestors" (Deuteronomy 30:1–5).

"And the Lord God made clothing from animal skins for Adam and his wife" (Genesis 3:21).

"So I tell you, don't worry about everyday life—whether you have enough food to eat or clothes to wear, for life consists of far more than food and clothing. Look at the ravens. They don't need to plant or harvest or put food in barns because God feeds them, and you are far more valuable to him than any birds" (Luke 12:22–23).

1. Should we consume animals to live? Should other animals consume each other?
2. Will God bring punishment upon our nation if we fail to be obedient?
3. Are you afraid of aging?
4. Do we get more fearful if we live closer and closer together?
5. Fear is a necessary emotion, but don't we need to be thoughtful about what to fear?
6. Should we fear bringing children into the world? Wasn't the world more dangerous in the Middle Ages? If people feared bringing children in their world, then we might not be here today.
7. When does legitimate fear turn into neurotic fear? When we look at everything as something that may harm us, is it neurosis?

"The only thing we have to fear, is fear itself."—Franklin D. Roosevelt

Lucy: "Maybe you have pantophobia."
Charlie Brown: "What is that?"
Lucy: "The fear of everything."
Charlie Brown: "That's it!"—Charles Schultz, *Peanuts*

For the Love of God, Get Ready

Question: How do you start each day?

Some of us enjoy that first cup of coffee, while watching TV news. Some may read the Bible and say prayers. Some may just sit and ponder problems and plan for the day. Some may quietly listen to music; others may hit the ground running with a quick cup of coffee, a little breakfast, then off to get things done. Whatever our routine for starting the day and whatever our plans, the day often presents something unexpected. The unexpected things are just life being lived. If we are wise, we try to equip ourselves mentally, physically, and spiritually to deal with the unexpected. Unfortunately, many people don't even think about the importance of mental education, physical education, and most of all spiritual education. Many of us try to do only what we are forced to do by parents, teachers, or government and end up poorly prepared to face the world. Most of us think that a few years of school, playing a few sports, and going to Sunday school are all we need to last a lifetime.

I often use the analogy of a three-legged stool. One leg is mental, one is physical, and the third is spiritual. If we do not try to strengthen each leg that supports our lifetime efforts, we will eventually fall on our rears. Let us go over all three of these supporting aspects:

The mind is only as good as the information fed into the brain. Good parenting gives anyone a good start. There was a simple book a few years ago titled *All I Really Need to Know I Learned in Kindergarten*.(Author Robert Fulghum). It said that the principles of kindness, fairness, discipline, and respect are the foundation for a good life. What we fail to understand is that education does not end with a diploma; it should be a lifetime process.

The aging process is not something we can defeat; however, we can slow it down by regular exercise and proper nutrition. Fast food not only fails to provide the nutrition needed for maintaining good healthy bodies and minds, but it takes away the educational process of family dinners. Even family dinners can fail to provide learning and family togetherness if we let electronic devices control us. Leave the cell phones and TVs off at mealtime. A variety of vegetables, fruits, and protein sources are necessary. We sometimes provide our houseplants better nutrition than we do our family.

Spiritual education is connected to mental education, in that the spirit can only function well if we let it grow in God's love. We do this by reading, listening, and meditating. Our spirit grows by our love for each other and thereby our love for God. As we learn to love each other more, we allow the spirit of God to be one with our spirit. Meditation (quiet thinking) on God's presence in the world is the best food for our soul.

Many women take a lot of time putting themselves together correctly. They are constantly primping, adjusting, and brushing on the way to an event. We should learn something from those seemingly mundane acts. Life needs constant adjusting and grooming.

Start each day by thinking of God speaking to us through a good parent, saying, "For the love of God, get ready." Our Lord advised us to build good foundations so that we can face the world's storms.

"So why do you call me 'Lord' when you won't obey me? It is like a person who builds a house on a strong foundation laid upon the underlying rock. When the floodwaters rise and break against the house, it stands firm because it is well built. But anyone who listens and doesn't obey is like a person who builds a house without a foundation. When the floods sweep down against that house, it will crumble into a heap of ruins" (Luke 7:46–49).

1. Should not the first thing we do in the beginning of each day be to seek God's help in tending and repairing our foundation?
2. God will speak to us, but we cannot hear him if we are talking. Do you listen to God each morning?
3. We cannot clean our home once and expect it to stay clean, so why do we expect our souls to remain clean without tending?
4. Eating properly one day a week will not build a healthy body, so why do we think going to church one day a week will provide a healthy spirit?
5. If we think we know everything, we are not open to learning. Do you know someone who thinks he knows it all?
6. A good way to start your day is by the little habit of making your bed. Do you ever think, *No one is going to be here but me, so why should I make my bed?*

Recognizing God's presence is a good foundation for building a good day.

For the Love of God

Question: Have you ever wondered, how can I show my love to a God I cannot see or have never met? Why did Jesus have to die? How did that atone for my sins?

My wife took Reed, our three-year-old grandson, to a kindergarten program at Holy Rosary Church last month. Reed and Mary were there to watch his sister perform with her class. Reed began a series of questions for Grandma as he quickly observed the statues and crucifixes around him. Finally, his eyes got big and he said out loud, "Is that God? Is that blood on his hands?"

"Yes," Grandma replied softly.
"Why does he have blood? Does it hurt? Why?"

Good questions, and we all have wondered if we as adults can give a good answer.

Lent is the season of prayer and preparation for the most important holy day of Christianity, Easter. Ash Wednesday takes place forty days before Easter, but most Christians let it pass without much thought, prayer, or supplication. Many are only concerned with chocolate bunnies. During these forty days, we are encouraged to repent. On Ash Wednesday, we sometimes have ashes placed upon our foreheads to start Lent by remembering that we were dust and will return to dust. In the past, Christians fasted during the week to remind themselves of Christ's sacrifice and then feasted on Sundays to remember the joy of his resurrection. Few follow this tradition today, but I believe it would be a good thing to regenerate as we try to learn to love our God.

Christ sacrificed himself to atone for our sinful nature and to show us the ultimate way to show love. Our loving Father offers his holy grace to protect all of his children who will accept it, offering the gift of eternal life with Jesus just by believing, which brings with it our love for God and other people (John 1:29).

Scripture says that we were made in the image of God. We love God by loving each other. The only logical reason for our existence is to learn how to love God by loving each other. One way we love each other is to help others better understand Christ's message. The message brought by Jesus to this world was simple: "Love your God with all your heart, all your mind, and all your soul" (Luke 10:27). The second message is to love each other as we love ourselves.

People are perpetually tempted to create governance at the top of our civil and spiritual lives, which we allow to tell us what and how to think. This process can be harmful to our individual growth and responsibility. We have seen this in our increased dependence on our civil government's growth. We often allow our spiritual lives to weaken, giving up our inner relationship with the Holy Spirit and letting our church governing bodies describe in finite detail what constitutes a good Christian. We all have been promised by Jesus that the Holy Spirit will provide knowledge and wisdom and strength to see how to love our God (John 16:13).

Governing bodies are necessary in a civil society and in our Christian churches; however, we should be vigilant and not allow them to control our thinking. The ability to love our God and others comes from within each of us by the presence of the Holy Spirit. The Pharisees in Jesus's time became so involved in rules and regulations, they failed to see what was really important to God. Christ's message was simple; why do we always need to complicate it?

So what does it mean that God is love? Love is an attribute of God. Love is a core aspect of God's character, his person. Everything God does is loving, just as everything he does is just and right. God gave us the perfect example of love in Jesus and thereby gives us the ability to love as he does, through the power of the Holy Spirit.

In John 15:13, Jesus tells us that the greatest love is shown when people lay down their lives for their friends. That is what he did to show us his love for each of us. Let us keep that simple fact in our minds and hearts as we enter the period of prayer and supplication known as Lent, beginning on Ash Wednesday. I think that we can please our Father by not only prayer and meditation but by simple acts of love and kindness each day. Small acts of kindness will grow into great things we may not even see.

"I have loved you even as the Father has loved me. Remain in my love. When you obey me, you remain in my love, just as I obey my Father and remain in his love. I have told you this so that you will be filled with my joy. Yes, your joy will overflow! I command you to love each other in the same way that I love you. And here is how to measure it: The greatest love is shown when people lay down their lives for their friends. You are my friends if you obey me. I no longer call you servants, because a master doesn't confide in his servants. Now you are my friends, since I have told you everything the Father told me. You didn't choose me, I chose you. I appointed you to go and produce fruit that will last, so that the Father will give you whatever you ask for, using my name. I command you to love each other" (John 15:9–17).

1. Can we lay down our lives for friends without giving up our earthly lives?
2. Do you sometimes think the church hierarchy makes rules concerning moral values that you do not agree with?
3. We let our government tell us which side of the street to drive on; how is it different if we give our church governance over our thoughts and actions?
4. Just as some of the rules and regulations of the Pharisees were valuable and some were silly or even harmful, can some laws today be harming us?
5. Do you personally spend time trying to understand love?

6. Just as our civil government can change the original intent of a law by writing new regulations, do you think our church does the same thing?
7. Will you commit to doing an act of kindness each day during Lent?

"I believe what we all would find deep in our hearts is a desire to love and be loved. It is natural in childhood and sometime buried in adulthood."—James Dille, *Questions*

Friendship

Question: Do you have any old friends you have lost contact with?

I was talking to a customer at my pharmacy last week, and during the conversation, I realized that I had worked with his mother years ago. I didn't remember much about her, except that she was a nice lady. We talked for a while about where she had worked in the past, and I learned that she had worked for Louie, a physician I knew thirty-five years ago. I had lost contact with him after he had moved back to Louisiana. I am constantly reminded of Louie whenever my knee hurts (he repaired it by surgery back then). During our conversation, the customer told me that Louie had been dead for ten years, killed in a private plane crash. It was shocking to hear he was dead but even more disquieting to think that I thought about him all these years, believing he was safely practicing orthopedics somewhere. I remembered a night spent with Louie and another friend, cooking a whole hog for a barbeque contest. My only contribution had been the story I told the judges about the life of the pig we had cooked. I created a story that Tobie had been raised by a loving Mennonite family which had fed him pecans, which gave him his unique flavor. Amazement filled Louie's face as my tall tale was being created before his eyes and ears. We won grand championship and an invite to Memphis in May contest, that spring.

Over the years, I have tried to reconnect with many old friends; occasionally, I've been successful. Most of the time, I failed to find an old friend and now wonder how many of them are already with Jesus. I would guess that some of those old schoolmates from Rife Memorial Grade School are no longer in this world. I wonder about Wendell Miller. Did he get drafted and sent to some foreign land and lost his life years ago? Did he go away to college and is now CEO of a large corporation? I never saw him after that day because he didn't go to high school with us. Susan Jones, who was so smart and always won the spelling contests; did she perhaps become a writer? She may have married and had a child who became a famous author.

We can't keep in contact with everyone we once knew, but perhaps we should make more of an effort to contact certain people we had special relationships with. The traits we once found attractive are usually still part of their character.

These thoughts bring me to the question, what is a friend? I think that a friend is someone you share common interests with. A friend is someone you can share your most private thoughts, without fear of them hurting or judging you. A friend is someone you can sit with in silence without feeling that you must say something. Enjoying silence with a friend is a good time to bond even more. Friends sometimes just let you babble about nothing in particular, finding some enjoyment in your meandering thoughts. A friend is someone you can totally be who you are in front of. You can be grumpy, happy, sad, fearful, anxious, or however you feel without fear of judgment. A friend will let you tell old stories over and over, with a smile of enjoyment. Even though you get separated by space, time, and events, a friend is always there when you reconnect. Friendships do require effort and tending, just like a flower garden. A note or phone call now and then will keep your hand on your friend's shoulder, no matter how far away he or she is.

Ask yourself, What kind of a friend am I? There is a difference between knowing someone well and being a true friend. The greatest evidence of genuine friendship is loyalty. Think of your friends and assess your loyalty to them. True friends are there even when you are in the depth of sin and failure. Do not let friendships wither and die because you don't want to be seen as a friend of someone who has failed in life.

"Love is patient and kind. Love is not jealous or boastful or proud or rude. Love does not demand its own way. Love is not irritable, and it keeps no record of when it has been wronged. It is never glad about injustice but rejoices whenever the truth wins out. Love never gives up, never loses faith, is always hopeful, and endures through every circumstance" (1 Corinthians 13:4–7).

1. Why don't you call that friend who is in trouble?
2. Have you ever been given a lift by a friend's call?
3. Do you treat your friends like you would like to be treated?
4. Have you ever joined a conversation that belittles someone you considered a friend?
5. Have you ever abandoned a friend because he was sinning?

God and Our Brain (Seeking Inner Peace)

Question: Are you good at reading people? What are your methods?

When my daughter Ashley was about two years old, we were visiting my Uncle Lawrence, who seemed to have a permanent frown on his face. He had seen brutal combat during World War II and returned home to find that his wife had been unfaithful, so he should be forgiven for that countenance. On this day, Uncle Lawrence was somewhere else in his mind, unaware of his facial expression, but little Ashley noticed. She climbed onto my lap and asked, "Why hims mad?"

We all laughed, including Uncle Lawrence, bringing his more loveable nature to the front. I became more aware of my facial expressions because of that experience, but I'm still am unable to completely control them when in deep thought. I believe my uncle could not calm the unresolved troubles in his inner self. He eventually took his own life.

In his book *The Brain*, David Eagleman teaches us how the brain communicates with itself by billions of neuronal connections and also how we connect with each other in ways heretofore not fully understood. Eagleman describes an experiment using a transcranial magnetic stimulator (TMS), which creates magnetic pulses outside the brain that stimulate and activate neurons inside the brain. A young man in the experiment was within the autism spectrum, with a diagnosis of Asperger's. John was unaware of certain aspects of the social world until after being exposed to TMS pulses in the area of his brain that was involved with reading other's signals. He was unable to interpret facial expressions and body language we utilize in socialization. After being exposed to the TMS, his brain made connections that changed his world. Weeks after the exposure to TMS, he could see that there were messages emanating from the facial expressions of others. The magnetic pulse unlocked something in his brain.

We humans have an ability to empathize with others in many ways, but one way is by mirroring their facial expressions. When someone smiles at us, we tend to smile back. It is true with all emotional facial expressions. Anger also gets mirrored; our brain machinery picks up the facial expression we have created to tell us to become angry also.

We have been created to assess our surroundings by picking up signals that are visible, but our brains produce impulses that may be read subconsciously by other brains. It is interesting that couples that live together for a long time often begin to look alike. This is because after years of mirroring, we develop certain lines in our face from unconscious communications. I believe my wife reads my mind before I realize I am thinking something (but I hope she doesn't eventually look like me).

Most of us understand body language to a certain extent. We understand that if someone is leaning toward us and looking us in the eye, they probably are interested in what we are saying. If they are busy with their smartphone, however, they are probably not too interested in what we have to say.

In another experiment described in *The Brain*, babies less than one year old were shown a video while being held by their mothers. The simple video showed two bears and a duck. The bears had on different colored shirts and were watching the duck trying to open the lid on a box of toys. One of the bears saw the duck struggling and moved to help open the lid. After the lid was opened, displaying the toys, the other bear jumped on the lid, slamming it shut. After the video, each baby was offered a choice of the bears to play with, and they all chose the one that helped the duck. It seems that we are born with an ability to make judgments about the trustworthiness of others.

Scientists suggest that computers may someday be able to copy our brain in a manner that will support a functioning mind. It does not seem to matter if the software is supported by organic neurons or by silicone chips, if the arrangement, connections, and signal strength are reproduced. If this becomes possible and your mind, thoughts, memories are transferred to this hardware, will it be you? Will it be conscious? Will it think and have emotions? Will it have inner peace? Are the sensing elements of the body necessary for the mind to be conscious? Perhaps there is an element the scientists are ignoring: the spirit that emanates from God. The spirit, the essence of life, the soul cannot be measured by human intelligence.

We seem to have things going on in our brains that are God given. Some of these are necessary for us to live in this world. Our instinct to judge trustworthiness enables us to love. Without trust, love cannot exist. We should be more aware of our facial expressions, body language, and tone of voice. If we fail to even think of our body language or tone of voice, we may develop habits that produce poor communication with those we love.

Our human need to be with others in social contact requires us to be aware of our God and the spiritual energy emanating from him through each of us. When we are in harmony with God's will, we send more signals of the love that connects us to him. Keeping in touch with God all through the day helps us become harmonious with his will and helps us send more positive body language and spiritual language, showing that inner peace we were left by Jesus.

We can only find inner peace by accepting forgiveness through Christ's sacrifice and then forgiving everyone we ask for our forgiveness. If the transgressor does not seek our forgiveness, then release it to God (sometimes *release* is a better word than *forgiveness*).

"I am leaving you with a gift—peace of mind and heart. And the peace I give isn't like the peace the world gives. So don't be troubled or afraid" (John 14:27).

1. Do you have any unresolved issues that show on your face?
2. Do you have trouble letting go of the past and learning from it?

3. Have you ever had someone ask you what's wrong when you are in deep thought?
4. Do you appear to be looking more like your spouse or more like your dog?
5. Do you believe what is in your heart shows on your face?
6. Don't you find it more enjoyable to be around someone who smiles a lot than someone who frowns a lot?

Peace is not the absence of trouble; it is the presence of God.

Faith versus Intellect

Question: Have you ever had faith that God would answer your prayers, but he didn't?

Years ago, I had a very close friend who was facing death. His heart was failing. He had many people praying for him, me included. I told God that I would go to church every Sunday for a year if he would heal him. Seemed easy enough; however, it wasn't. One time, I was on a golf trip and had to leave my buddies to find a church in town; they ridiculed me. I was in a city with friends once and had to leave them in search of a church, causing hurt feelings. I sometimes went to a church of a different denomination. My pledge was not as easy as it seemed. I knew God did not require sacrifice, but sometimes, we can see something about our own sincerity by offering a sacrifice with a prayer. Our prayers were answered, and our friend lived several more years after receiving a heart transplant. Because of this little answered prayer, my faltering faith grew stronger.

Recently, I prayed for another friend, who was suffering from lung cancer. I asked God just to give him a little more time in this world because he was doing so much for broken people. I again offered a little sacrifice with my prayer and had faith that God would answer. I felt that I was to do something I really didn't want to do to fulfill my offering. I accepted that unpleasant challenge I thought God wanted and continued to have faith, but my friend soon died.

Why did God answer my faithful prayer the first time, but the second time, he seemed to say no? Most Christians experience similar negative responses from God from time to time, even if we have faith. I don't have any more insight than other Christians; however, I do have some thoughts I'd like to share.

God has a way of inspiring humankind without an audible voice. His voice goes beyond language itself. Understanding is something we are capable of, up to a point, and after our limits, we are asked to have faith. Faith is something that many people do not want to depend upon because it somehow tells them they are incapable of understanding everything. Some people can't admit they have limits to their intellect. God tells us that unless we become as little children, we will not enter into the kingdom of heaven. We have to admit our dependence upon faith. Little children submit to the wisdom and support provided by their parents and have faith they will provide that wisdom and support.

Faith can be fed by intellect, which means that God wants us to use our brains and intelligence to study, observe, and listen in order to create a mind-set that will allow faith to grow along with information to find God's omnipresence. If we seek God, he will reveal himself in ways only we can understand. We are all unique, and God understands that uniqueness. There is only one you; your intellectual being is unique. Our spiritual being is not unique; it is one with the Holy Spirit, if we accept God's love. The key to that acceptance is a combination of intellectual development that understands the requirement of faith.

There is only one thing that does not require faith, and that is when someone denies the existence of God. To deny God is to deny one's own existence. We only exist because of love, and God is love.

Jesus was sent to us to show us how to live. He taught us about love and all the things that love entails. He taught us about forgiveness, tolerance, steadfastness, prayer, and many other things that are all connected to love. The most difficult thing he taught about was faith.

On the night of his betrayal and arrest, Jesus struggled in the garden with his humanly faith. He told his disciples, "My soul is deeply grieved, to the point of death; remain here and keep watch with me."

His humanness was struggling with faith. He didn't get the answer his human side prayed for, and yet by faith, he accepted what was going to happen. His disciples seemed to fail him that night. Peter, James, and

John had the opportunity to prove their faith, yet they failed the test. Jesus found them sleeping and told them, "The spirit is willing but the flesh is weak." He returned to pray again, saying, "My Father, if this cannot pass away unless I drink it, Your will be done." (Matt 26:41)

Like Peter, James, and John, we often wonder if we did all that we could have done. We ask ourselves, "Did I have enough faith?" Some things are only answered by faith. Sometimes, we demand God answer our desires instead of saying, "Thy will be done." Sometimes, we become angry, just like Simon Peter, who drew a sword and slashed off the right ear of M

alchus. We think, *God isn't working this out the way I want it worked out.*

Jesus said to Peter, "Put your sword back into its sheath. Shall I not drink from the cup the Father has given me?" Like Peter, we get angry at circumstances and even God, saying, "I had the faith you wanted me to have, and this still happened."

Unfortunately, some of us seem to have a heavier burden than others; at least we as individuals think this is so. I believe we were taught by Jesus to keep remembering, "Not my will but thine be done." We are unable to understand some things about this life because of the limits of our intellect; we are told to accept them by faith. We are even told to accept our understanding of faith by faith. When we are tempted to take matters into our own hands, we must trust God. If Peter had had his way, Jesus would not have gone to the cross, and God's plan of redemption would have been thwarted.

When things are going well, we feel elated. When hardships come, we sink into depression. But true joy transcends the rolling waves of circumstance. Joy comes from a consistent relationship with Jesus Christ.

"I have told you this so that you will be filled with my joy. Yes, your joy will overflow" (John 15:11).

1. What do you do when your faith falters?

2. Do you ever get mad because you think your prayer went unanswered, even though you had faith?
3. Was Adam's sin about man demanding to know things that only God knows?
4. Is faith sometimes about accepting burdens we don't want to carry?
5. During Lent, will you pray for faith to accept your unique burdens, or will you complain to God that life is unfair?
6. Will you accept the fact that you are unable to understand everything?

Good Vibrations

Question: Do you have a song you would like to be sung at your funeral?

Everything in nature vibrates. The smallest particles are constantly moving in a seemingly defined rhythm. The source of our energy, the sun's rays, are vibrating particles that somehow produce the vibrations necessary for life on earth. It cannot be denied that these are good vibrations.

In the beginning, God struck a note, and our very purpose is to seek harmony with that note. Harmony produces a pleasing effect, and that is why God wants us to seek it in all aspects of this life. When our body is not in a healthy state, it is because certain cells are in disharmony. When individuals and families are dysfunctional, it is because they are in disharmony, and the same is true for nations. When radio waves are out of sync, static is produced. Disharmony is unpleasant in every aspect.

In some way, all of life is seeking some harmony after the Big Bang. All disciplines seem to be flowing in the same direction, whether it be mathematics, music, biology, poetry, or philosophy. They seem to want to piece together knowledge in a rhythm that flows to a common goal, and I believe that is God. I believe that the harmony of music is an audible manifestation of the harmonic perfection we seek with God. Most people who have had a near-death experience recall music that is all encompassing as they approach what must be the throne of God. They also speak of the colors being indescribably brilliant, beautiful, and soothing. Some people say everything produces this music of God, even the flowers and grass. There is complete harmony, and that is the pure love that envelops everything. It seems to me that anything that is producing love, whether it is sensual or spiritual, is godly and therefore necessary in God's realm.

The universe was created using the tools of music, harmony, and balance. Everything is kept in place by God's all-pervading vibrations. The music heard by those that have had near-death experiences is described as sublimely beautiful, with harmonic perfection.

Dr. Eben Alexander, author of *Proof of Heaven,* describes an orb of white light emitting an indescribable melody that accompanied his view of heaven. After drifting away from the higher place, he could recall this melody and re-enter the heavenly realm. People who have had near death experiences repeat this same description of beautiful music, color, and love.

In his book, Dr. Alexander tells us "we must all understand that the real consciousness is separate from our brain and body and it is what is interconnecting all of us, and is also our connection with God." We can touch that consciousness by prayer and meditation, putting aside our ego, which wants to interfere in an earthly way and keep us from communicating with our creator, who unconditionally loves us. When we attain that level of consciousness, we are really in harmony with God. Music helps us get into that spiritual state.

In this state of consciousness, God speaks to us in ways that we should pay attention to. We should not ignore the seemingly insignificant communications from God when we allow our spirit, our soul, to open to his voice. Heaven is around us now, if we are open to experiencing the unconditional love emanating from it and surrounding all of us.

After the apostle John became open to the message God, he wanted to tell everyone about the full identity of Christ and to give warning and hope to believers. He tells us what was revealed to him about music in heaven:

"Then I looked again, and I heard the singing of thousands and millions of angels around the throne and the living beings and the elders. And they sang in a mighty chorus" (Revelation 6:11).

1. If God didn't think music was important, why did he devote a whole book to the psalms of David?
2. Do you ever listen to music to change your mood?

3. Does the sound of children singing fill your heart with love?
4. Can you praise our Lord without music?
5. Do you remember what song was sung at your wedding?

"Give me some music, moody food of us that trade in love."—Cleopatra, in Shakespeare's *Antony and Cleopatra*

"Aside from love, music is the most powerful force in the universe."—Garth Brooks

Happiness and Unhappiness

Question: What would a happy day be like for you? What would an unhappy day be like? Would it be similar to a happy or unhappy day when you were young?

When I was young, I thought I was happiest when I was anticipating something that would bring me pleasure. I was unhappy when I had nothing to look forward to. As an adult, I sometimes think I am happy when I am not feeling stress over various issues; perhaps stress of anticipating an event I was committed to that I really didn't want to be a part of. Perhaps stress of anxiety about something that required an expense of energy. I am unhappy when I must do something I really don't want to do. It appears that presence or anticipation of stress is one of the defining elements of happiness as an adult. As a young person, happiness was more positive anticipation. Unhappiness was the absence of anticipation.

If stress is an important element of unhappiness as an adult and if you underwent the steps to eliminate most of the stress-causing events, people, jobs, mosquitos, or anything that stresses you, what would your life be like? Let's see: you won't have any children, grandchildren, puppies, or a job. Will you be happy then? No, in fact, most of us would be very unhappy to eliminate everything in our lives that we take pleasure in.

Okay, here in my old age, I am beginning to understand what happiness was, is, and will be. Happiness was the same as a child as it is as a young adult, a middle-aged adult, or an older person. It is not a birthday gift, Christmas toy, new automobile, big house, expensive suit. No, it is not things, big or small, inexpensive or expensive. Happiness is about love: first, love of oneself and love of family, friends, and animals, thereby loving our Lord. When I look back, it was those little things that I took no notice of that made me happy, like sitting on a step in my grandmother's kitchen, watching her cook and listening to her stories. Happiness was watching my dad sitting in his chair, smiling as he watched his grandsons wrestle. It's watching my little girls playing house, acting like they were their mother and her friend across the street; these were happy moments. Happiness was listening to my young son and his friends as they played football in a vacant field. Happiness was having my mother's blue eyes fixed upon me after I was ready for school, as if she thought I was special. Happiness is when I look around my clean house and notice that there are clean socks in my drawer. Happiness is when I am laughing with a friend. Happiness is laughing with Mary and feeling pride when I look at her dressed up for an event, because I know she'll be the prettiest one there. Happiness is enjoying a cup of hot coffee in the morning and talking with her about silly things, or perhaps about God. Happiness is enjoying my grandchildren doing little things and watching Mary's eyes light up with a phone call from the grandkids or telling me about something they did.

Unhappiness is the absence of love. It is when you cannot recognize those little things that God blesses us with. Unhappiness is gossiping about people, passing along things we hear that make others appear smaller than us in some way. Some people like to point out other people's bad choices and mistakes. My dad seldom would join in such critical conversations developed, unless it was criticizing President Hoover, who he thought caused the Depression. I've tried to be like him but have fallen short. Unhappiness is envy, hatred, fear. Unhappiness is not putting Jesus first in our life.

I find it difficult to dislike people. I may dislike their behavior, if they do something that harms another person. Then I try to find a reason for their bad behavior. I have a list of people I should dislike, according to other people's opinions. If I try to dislike someone because someone tells me I should, I feel bad (that is, unless it is someone of the other political party).

"Do not judge others, and you will not be judged. Do not condemn others or it will all come back against you. Forgive others, and you will be forgiven. Give, and you will receive. Your gift will return to you in full—pressed down, shaken together to make room for more, running over and poured into your lap. The amount you give will determine the amount you get back" (Luke 6:37–38).

"For the despondent, every day brings trouble. For the happy heart, life is a continual feast" (Proverbs 15–15).

1. Have you ever failed to be kind to someone because someone else expected it of you?
2. There is a difference between forgiveness and release. Is *release* a better word for those who don't ask for forgiveness?
3. Can you remember those small things that made you happy in the past? Do they make you happy today?
4. Do you sometimes let worry about tomorrow steal your happiness today?
5. Do you believe the happiest words in the world are "I love you"?

Heaven

Question: What do you think heaven will be like? Will the streets be paved with gold? Will we know other people there? Will your uncle you loved but never became a Christian be there?

We all wonder what heaven will be; our vision of the next life has probably changed as we grew old. I would guess that those who believe in an afterlife as a place of joy, peace, and comfort promised by Jesus have some vision of what the next life will be like. We only have scriptures to go on. I therefore know nothing personally about what I am going to talk about. I will qualify my words to follow with "This is how I would like it to be, and I pray that the Lord in his infinite wisdom will not take my advice, at least if my ideas subtract from his perfection."

We seem to be given little glimpses of heaven when people experience near-death events. There have been many books written by people who have begun that voyage and been given a view, only to be turned back at the last minute. Many books tell of bright lights and brilliant colors as they go down a passageway from this life to the next. Often there are relatives there to greet them and serve as guides. Oftentimes, people in their spiritual passage see or feel the presence of Jesus. Everyone speaks of the overwhelming feeling of love. There is an understanding that comes with any question just by the blending of our souls with that presence of love. We will cease to question; we will understand by our personal relationship with God. Our personal spiritual tank will be full; though those tanks may vary in capacity, they will all be full of love and knowledge without any jealousy, envy, resentment, anger, fear, or anxiety.

Heaven will be pain free, and our ability to fully feel love will be uninhibited by fragile bodies or brains that limit us in earth time. We will not be limited by space or time because both would limit our sensitivity in the complete life of heaven. We'll no longer fear disease or danger, and we'll experience God's heaven. We will not be limited to the five senses we have on earth; we can only imagine complete sensitivity of the heavenly environment and experiences. Imagine more colors and sounds of music provided by our loving God that only amplify our sensitivity to love. We will be aware of earthly negative emotions only to be totally aware of their absence in the presence of our Lord. We can only imagine the joy to come by perhaps comparing it to the birth of a baby as it becomes aware of the new life full of light, color, smells, tastes, and feelings; love causes that newborn baby to look into its loving mother and father's eyes, offering its first smile. Nothing honors parents more than that first smile brought to them, perhaps, from a heavenly connection; God's gift of a baby reconnects them to the heavenly realm.

As I sit here trying to see the unseen, my back is aching. I can only see the beauty of the outside through worn-out eyes and a small window in my office. Likewise, I can barely hear the joyful sounds of spring birds because of my hearing loss. I can only smell the fragrances of flowers at a lesser intensity. I feel a little anxious about grass that needs mowing and bills that need to be paid. I am pained by these thoughts in constant conflict with my humanly endeavor to be positive. I worry about my sick friends and those pained by the loss of loved ones and other tragedies. Comfort is provided by faith and prayer for more faith. My prayer is not for absence of pain and tragedy but for strength to endure, endure until I am guided to that place of complete love we refer to as heaven. That endurance is made easier by the understanding that even in tragedy, good can result, if we learn that God wants us to focus on what we have left, not on what we lost.

"For to be carnally minded is death, but to be spiritually minded is life and peace" (Romans 8:6).

"For by grace you have been saved through faith, and that not of yourselves; it is the gift of God, not of works, lest anyone should boast" (Ephesians 2:8–9).

"For I am persuaded that neither death nor life, nor angels nor principalities nor powers, not things present nor things to come, nor height nor depth, nor any other created thing, shall be able to separate us from the love of God which is in Christ Jesus our Lord" (Romans 8:38–39).

"But if you won't believe me when I tell you about things that happen here on earth, how can you possibly believe if I tell you what is going on in Heaven?" (John 3:12).

1. Why don't we rejoice more when sending a loved one to be with Jesus?
2. Where does a baby's first smile come from (certainly not from this life's experiences)?
3. In a place of existence which only allows love, doesn't everything else take care of itself?
4. Is accepting the love of Christ all we are asked to do in order to receive eternal life?
5. You can't have something you won't accept; will those who don't accept Jesus's love have eternal life?
6. Just as a new baby is a new creation, isn't everyone in Christ a new creation?
7. Does heaven begin when we accept Jesus Christ? Is accepting the love of Christ accepting him?

"If someone thinks that love and peace is a cliché that must have been left behind in the sixties, that's his problem. Love and peace are eternal."—John Lennon

The longing to understand will be fulfilled in our new life, not limited by the confines of space and time.

Here I Am, Lord

Question: Should your church fit your needs, or should you fit your church's needs? Is it sometimes better to move on to find a church that fits you better?

Let's say you've finished your earthly Christian experience and stand before our Lord; would you say something like the following?

"Here I am, Lord, standing in your presence. I have usually kept your commandments, except a few. I have worshiped you with prayer, song, and scriptures. I have loved my church by gifts and works. Oh yes, it was not my church; it was your church. Well, I did what I could to tend to your flock and see that they were guided toward you. I have taught love, except a few times. I have taught tolerance, except a few times. I have forgiven and taught forgiveness, except a few times. I am proud that when a man came to your church to worship you who was dirty, I told him to leave. He had no business standing at the front of the church because he was not clean, and he wore dirty clothing. I asked him to leave that day, even though he said he only wanted to worship you. I felt he was distracting to the flock, and I knew him to be a sinful drunk against your scriptures (Ephesians 5:18). I felt good about that, and I felt good about myself. I also asked the women to not speak in church because 1 Corinthians 14:34 says it's the right thing to do. I asked all the divorced people to leave the church because I thought your scriptures told me it was wrong to divorce (Matthew 19:9). I asked openly gay people not to serve because your scriptures told me it was wrong (1 Timothy 1:10). I told everyone who was living in sin with someone, without the blessings of marriage, to not have any leadership role because I read in the scriptures that the elders should be exemplary (Titus 1:5–9). Sometimes, I didn't want to tell the truth about things in my church because I didn't want to hurt anyone's feelings, and I didn't want to serve on committees myself because I can't make them see my way. I didn't feel inspired by that one pastor and tried to get him removed for the benefit of the church. Yes, Lord, I tried to tend your flock, but I noticed that no one was left to help me. Oh yes, there was that one church that would not forgive me for a mistake I made, even though I asked you for forgiveness. I never liked all the division in that church. That's why I moved to another church."

Or would you fall down before the Lord and say something like the following:

"Forgive me, oh Lord, for I was a sinner. I fell short of your expectations and failed you in so many ways. I didn't try to harmonize with your love, as you asked. I asked for you to harmonize with me, instead. I found fault in others and praised my own success, failing to see your gifts to me. I often disrupted your church instead of working within to create harmony with your love. I looked at the failures of others instead of at my own. I only looked to scriptures for guidance, failing to see your presence within myself for some guidance. I failed to be open to anyone else's ideas of truth. I know now that the only truth on earth can be found through your Holy Spirit's guidance and faith in your grace. I humbly fall before you, asking forgiveness promised through your grace and the blood of my savior, Jesus."

"But now when I mention this next issue, I cannot praise you. For it sounds as if more harm than good is done when you meet together. First of all, I hear that there are divisions among you when you meet as a church, and to some extent I believe it. But, of course there must be divisions among you so that those of you who are right will be recognized!" (1 Corinthians 11:17–19).

"As God's messenger, I give each of you this warning: Be honest in your estimate of yourselves, measuring your value by how much faith God has given you. Just as our bodies have many parts and each part has a special function, so it is with Christ's body. We are all parts of his one body, and each of us has different work to do. And since we are all one body in Christ, we belong to each other, and each of us needs all the others" (Romans 12:3–5).

1. Is it best to move to another church if the one you have been attending does not seem to be fulfilling your ideals?
2. Do you tend to think your ideas are usually right and if others would only think like you, the world would be a better place?
3. Have you ever wanted to leave a church because you didn't like some of the people there?
4. Do you do what you think God wants you to help your church grow in his spirit?
5. Do you ever think certain people in your church are sinning and therefore should not be working within the leadership?
6. Have you ever thought that your gifts to your church were misused or unappreciated?
7. Is God's grace only for certain sinners and sins?

"One may tolerate a world of demons for the sake of an angel."—Steven Moffat

"Tolerance becomes a crime when applied to evil."—Thomas Mann

"Resolve to be tender with the young, compassionate with the aged, sympathetic with the striving, and tolerant with the weak and wrong. Sometime in your life, you have been all of these."—Gautama Buddha

Humiliation

Question: Can you remember a time you felt humiliated? Was it caused by a perpetrator, self-inflected, or an act of nature? What was your response?

Humiliation is an emotion that is the root of many conflicts in our personal lives as well as in the world. The normal reaction to being humiliated is anger; repudiation or revenge often follow.

When I was in high school, my basketball coach slapped me in the face in front of the crowd during a game. I felt humiliated and still feel anger to this day about the asymmetrical relationship that allowed me to be unjustly punished and put down in front of everyone. My reaction was to quit the team for the rest of my junior year. My seventeen-year-old pride required me to do something. I sometimes wish that I had punched the coach in the face. This would have been a bad reaction, I'm afraid; I would have been suspended from school for sure. There was another factor involved; the coach was a former boxer.

When I was about six years old, I decided that spitting at my brother was a good way to respond when I was angry. Finally, after many attempts to correct my behavior, my mother called me to stand in front of her. After I did as she requested, she spat in my face. I was shocked and humiliated. Mom asked how it felt and then let me process the punishment. I stopped spitting on my brother.

I developed other methods to express my anger. Throwing rocks became a pretty good way to express my displeasure at my brother. I also created a trap in the woods on the way to Grandma's house. I propped a brick over the path with a trip vine that would make the brick fall onto his head. My plan to conk my older brother failed because the next day, I was the first one to run down the path; I forgot about the vine and tripped the trap. The corner of the brick landed on top of my head. I retain the scar to remind me of my foolish behavior.

One time, I was with a group of men laughing as two men teased a mentally deficient young man. I failed to do the right thing and call for this abuse to stop. I just sat quietly like the rest of the group, some of whom were enjoying the ridicule.

We may only be embarrassed and then let our own mind make us feel humiliated. But to be humiliated, I think we are made to feel less of a person. We are shown to be less valuable as a human being, or our own mind allows us to feel devalued, degraded, lowered in the eyes of others.

I wonder if terrorists have felt humiliation, and their response to this feeling of degradation in the eyes of the world is to lash out with murderous violence. When someone punches you in the nose, you feel better when you respond the same way. If you think about most of the world conflicts, humiliation is a factor. Hitler felt humiliated by Germany's loss of World War I. He felt the root cause of the country's loss was the Jewish race. Genocide was his reaction.

We recently experienced a presidential election in which many were surprised while some were humiliated by the results. The establishment has reacted to that feeling of humiliation with anger, as did many citizens who wanted a different result. The other side may have reacted in like manner if the election results had been different. Information from teachers, news people, and politicians have a huge effect upon reactions. There is a feeling of impotence after losing which, may be the beginning of a mind-set of humiliation, which calls for an angry response of some degree. Insult, injury, anger, shame, and how we process our feelings along with information will determine how we respond. When we get false information and have a tendency to feel insulted, shamed, and angry, we have a potentially explosive situation.

In personal relationships, if one person feels humiliated by a spouse, friend, or associate, the result often is the end of that relationship. Bullying is an attempt to make another person feel devalued and humiliated; many times, suicide is the result.

Mental deficiencies may be the reason some individuals are less equipped to deal with insults and the feeling of shame or inadequacy; however, lack of truthful information is often involved. Certain cultures are also more sensitive about saving face. We have to learn from parents, teachers, churches, and mentors to feel comfortable about who we are in order to react to the insults of this world in a healthy manner.

Our Lord Jesus Christ suffered the ultimate humiliation during his time on earth. There were insults by Jewish leaders, and he was tried unjustly with false witnesses, flogged, and hung on a cross naked to die before a crowd of people. Jesus never let any of these events make him feel humiliated.

"And so, dear brothers and sisters I plead with you to give your bodies to God. Let them be a living and holy sacrifice—the kind he will accept. When you think of what he had done for you, is this too much to ask? Don't copy the behavior and customs of this world, but let God transform you into a new person by changing the way you think. Then you will know what God wants you to do, and you will know how good and pleasing and perfect his will really is" (Romans 12:1–2).

1. Do you rely upon Jesus to help you deal with insults and belittlement?
2. Have you ever bullied someone or stood by as others did so?
3. Have you ever made your spouse or child feel humiliated?
4. Have you ever humiliated yourself?
5. Have you ever tried to humiliate an official at a sporting event?
6. The next time you feel the urge to attempt to humiliate someone, would it be good to remember how it feels?
7. What is the difference between humility and humiliation?
8. What is the difference between being embarrassed and being humiliated?

We should not feel humiliated by old age if we remember the love we've experienced getting old.

I'm Dreaming of a White Christmas

Question: How do you visualize in your mind the events that will make up your Christmas experience?

Visualization is how we form the future, whether we believe it or not. Sometimes we say, "I'll believe it when I see it," when we should say, "I believe it; therefore, I will see it."

Have you ever noticed a basketball player getting ready to shoot a free throw, utilizing visualization in a positive sense? The player stands with his toes on the line, waiting for the referee to throw him the ball, and he often takes a few seconds to go through the motions of shooting the ball and visualizing it going through the hoop. A baseball player does the same thing when he is waiting to go up to bat. He will look at the pitcher throwing the ball to the batter ahead of him and swing his bat as though he is up. In his mind, he is following a ball thrown to him and striking the ball in the manner he desires. I've watched my wife looking in a shop mirror, holding a dress in front of her body and visualizing how it will look at an upcoming party. We utilize the past to look into the future from the now to see where our next step should go.

The Christmas season is a great time to understand how visualization or dreaming brings good tidings. "The children were nestled all snug in their beds. While visions of sugar plums danced in their heads." This line from the famous poem *A Visit from St. Nicholas* is known by almost every American; we have all experienced those visions.

The Advent season is the period beginning four Sundays before Christmas, and is part of our Christian anticipation of something great getting ready to happen. This is one time during the year when almost all Christians feel a hint of the love of Christ that is always present. There are always a few Grinches or Scrooges around for those with a positive visualization of the upcoming events to help.

The Grinches and Scrooges who confront us during Advent should be looked upon as opportunities instead of obstacles. They give us all the opportunity to teach love and change miserable lives into more joyful ones.

The last Christmas I had with my paternal grandparents, I was taught a great lesson by my mom. It was going to be a wonderful event; I had dreamed of it while studying for finals at end of my first semester at St. Louis College of Pharmacy. My brother would be home from Southern Illinois University, and both grandmothers and the remaining grandfather would be there. I knew there would be good food and good fellowship. It was going to be great to be home for the first time in several months. I had been away from home for the first time and was really dreaming of a perfect Christmas. I had just bought a movie camera and filmed some of that day; almost sixty years later, I enjoy flooding my mind and soul with memories past. There are scenes of the night before that Christmas and some of Christmas morning, but there is one scene that brings a lesson about love home to me all these years later.

In my movie, one scene is of the whole family standing on our porch. Standing in the middle is an older woman with coke bottle glasses; it was Minnie Barent, who lived across the street, one house down from our two-story home. Ms. Barent was what we called an old maid in those days and someone the neighborhood boys would torment on Halloween. In fact, my mom and Aunt Frances did their share of laughing about Minnie. They often sat on our front lawn in summer evenings when windows were open and listened to Minnie rant to her ninety-five-year-old mother about the futility of life. She'd give a futility dissertation to her old mother, saying she didn't know why they bothered, "all you do is buy a pound of bologna one day and eat it just to pass it out the next day." Ms. Minnie also bothered Mom and Aunt Frances by singing a little off key in our choir at the church on the hill. She stood between the two each Sunday and, with a great deal of pride, belted out a nasal tone she thought was in harmony. We didn't understand then that singing in the choir with Mom and Aunt Frances was perhaps the most important thing in her life.

That Christmas in 1956, Minnie was living alone because her mother had passed away several years before, leaving her to live her life of despair without an audience. Mom, guided by a spirit of Christmas, invited Ms. Minnie to our dinner. I learned something about love, tolerance, and forgiveness that wonderful day, which I've never forgotten. Ms. Minnie treated my brother and me with a graciousness that was so contrary to what our youthful antics deserved. Her smiles and laughter that day told me that she loved us, in spite of the tormenting she got from ornery young boys.

A fifteen-year-old friend told me a few weeks ago that we all seek to be remembered. I will always remember a simple little lady made happy one Christmas by my mother.

Ms. Minnie is singing harmoniously in a heavenly choir now, with a voice she always visualized, standing among the armies of heaven and praising God with my mom and Aunt Frances.

"Glory to God in the highest heaven, and peace on earth to all whom God favors" (Luke 2:14).

1. When was the last time you tried to make the peace of Jesus available for someone?
2. Do you believe the only thing positive about anything negative is what you learn from it?
3. Are you able to forgive those who trespass against you?
4. Can you see the seemingly chaos of Christmas celebrations as perfection in the eyes of the Lord?
5. Have you ever been the Grinch who tried to steal Christmas? Why?
6. Will you do a small act of kindness this Christmas season? How about each day?

The small things we do in life are usually the big things.

Islam or Christianity

Question: Do you believe we can coexist with Islam?

There is a question of utmost importance presented to each of us daily by the press and TV news reports, but many of us just brush it aside. What should we as Christians be doing? Should we accept as a fact that the basic tenets of Islam are compatible with Christianity?

There are basic differences between Islam and Christianity that do not mesh. The Islam view of God, or Allah, is a supernatural being that does not always offer salvation, as Christians believe. Their Allah is not motivated by love but can be vicious and arbitrary in serving justice to humanity. Allah can change his mind for no apparent reason. Islamists believe they are saved by their acts and are never quite sure if they performed enough acts to please their Allah. They do think if they are martyred, they will be taken into a heaven with seventy-two virgins waiting to pleasure them. This very concept belittles women. They think that women are here to serve their needs and are not equal to men in Allah's eyes. Islamists believe that anyone who is not of their faith will be sent to an everlasting punishment in hell, where unbelievable torture will be waiting for them.

The belief by Islam that we are born good, versus Christianity's belief that we are guilty of original sin, is the only concept that may have merit in my mind. I believe that God gave all of us a brain capable of reason and also the capability of disbelief and rejection of God's love. I believe babies are born with a basic goodness as a gift of God and can learn to be evil and sin against God's love. The concept of original sin has been debated for centuries. Augustine expounded upon this concept, which was first developed by the bishop of Lyons in the second century, interpreting scriptures such as Romans 5:12–21. The belief of Augustine that all unbaptized infants went to hell makes me doubt his imprimatur of original sin. Things change in the world, and if we Christians never question our own beliefs, how can we challenge misguided interpretations of our relationship with God or Allah by Muslims?

A follower of Islam believes that there are basic acts prescribed by the Koran they must perform, such as praying five times a day while facing Mecca. They believe that certain foods are not to be consumed and others should only be eaten in a certain way. Christians believe that all we have to do is believe in God through the love of Jesus, and we are saved. This love will not allow sin. Sin is when we take something that we are not entitled to take. Whether it be another's self-respect, their possessions, their faith, or perhaps their life or their ability to pursue happiness. Islam allows all of this if the other person is not a Muslim.

There were ideologies in the past that may have seemed legitimate early on, but eventually, the world recognized the need to defeat them. The development of Nazism within a German nation that was basically good comes to mind. The world had to expose and defeat this philosophy. The misguided philosophies developing within Islam that are intolerant of other religions and threaten our existence should be exposed and defeated by force, if necessary. Tolerance of intolerance is in some ways the same as tolerance of evil.

What we Christians should do is first of all, strengthen our own faith and pray continually for the guidance of our Lord. Second, we should become informed by all information available and find truth through reason with educated and open minds, guided by faith in a loving God. Third, we should not let so-called political correctness prevent us from speaking out against those who want to eliminate our faith. We should understand that there are powerful forces in our world that are basically evil or motivated by something other than the love of God. These forces are sometimes presented by our own media in a way that appears to be neutral but has the net effect of destroying the faith in Jesus and God that our civilization and this melting pot, the United States, was founded upon. In the name of tolerance and neutrality, we can ignore what is going on, or we can just try to live our lives as we see fit, thinking that others will do the same and leave us alone. It seems that many in the Western culture we know have seen fit to be ignorant, which is to ignore.

It is interesting that we more often define ourselves by our packaging than our inner selves, our thoughts, and attitudes, basically our souls. I believe that our connection to God is through our souls, and these souls are informed by our experiences in life and by the grace of God. Jesus taught us that if we pray to strengthen our connection with God, we will be protected, not from danger but from the fear of danger.

I believe that God does not give us the intellect and physical power to survive and then expect us not to utilize it when we are in danger and facing death. He assures us that our souls will survive, but he does not expect all of us to become martyrs, giving up our earthly existence without a fight. This includes a fight for our faith as well as a fight for our lives.

Paul gave Timothy advice that serves all Christians well in his first letter to Timothy:

"Timothy, my son, here are my instructions for you, based on the prophetic words spoken about you earlier. May they give you the confidence to fight well in the Lord's battles. Cling tightly to your faith in Christ, and always keep your conscience clear. For some people have deliberately violated their consciences: as a result their faith has been shipwrecked" (1 Timothy 18:19).

1. Does God expect us to turn our other cheek when our faith is being assaulted by a friend or an enemy?
2. How can we juxtapose our instructions to turn our other cheek against the requirement to protect our families?
3. By keeping faith in our Lord, will we be protected from the evils of this world?
4. Should we welcome our Muslim brothers into our home, knowing that our faith will protect us?
5. Are we better off not getting into political or religious discussions?
6. What is the best way to convert a Muslim: by example or intellect or both?

Jesus: The Only Way

Question: If Jesus is the only way, do you wonder about little children who die before accepting him? Those who died in the womb? Those who were aborted? What about people who lived before Jesus, and what about people who live in faraway lands who never heard of Jesus? What about those who lived a life of love but never were saved?

My dad has been gone now for forty-five years, yet I still feel his presence. I still love him and still try to live up to the values he taught me. He went to church but never read the Bible. I do not know if he was saved, in the traditional sense. I can't see my dad, but I believe in his spiritual presence. My love for him transcends this earth, this time, and this space. I cannot see spirits or souls, but I believe they exist, and I believe my love for my dad was not so much love for his earthly body but for his essence. His was a life of love. By the same token, I do not love Jesus's earthly body, which I've never seen, but his godly quintessence.

We Christians believe in the Trinity, God in three persons. The Trinity is difficult to understand by our finite minds; however, we accept it as truth. Even though Jesus said, "The Father is greater than I" (John 14–28), we are taught the three are all God and somehow equal. Maybe an analogy would be to think of our government with the three coequal branches of legislative, judicial, and executive (God being the executive).

Jesus told the Pharisees he existed even before Abraham, causing them to become angry and confused. We were told that he existed throughout time. We as humans want to try to understand God; most of the time, we reduce him to human terms in the process. We try to understand his presence in our linear view of time. I believe what Jesus was saying is that God has always been. We are also told by scriptures that God is love; therefore, the Trinity, including Jesus, is love.

I am just a man and subject to error; however, I am free to study and use my mind and my own understanding of God's message while praying for the insight and clarity that come only from the Holy Spirit (John 16:13). It is my belief, therefore, that Jesus is love, and love has always existed since humanity's first breath and before. If we love each other, we love our Lord. If we love our Lord, we have his presence within us. If we love as God has instructed, no matter where in space or when in time, we accept Jesus because Jesus is God, and they are one with the Spirit, and they are all love.

"For God so loved the world that he gave his only Son, so that everyone who believes in him will not perish but have eternal life. God did not send his Son into the world to condemn it, but to save it" (John 3:16–17). I believe this means that Jesus did not come to find people to condemn but to bring an understanding of love, which would save us all.

We try to complicate it, but it's really quite simple: "Love your God with all your heart all your soul, all your mind. Then love your neighbor as you love yourself" (Matthew 22:39). It seems to me that if someone loves in this manner, they accept Jesus and are accepted into the Kingdom of God.

Whether Jews, Muslims, Hindus, Buddhists, Shinto, or whatever, it is ultimately God, not us, who will offer his grace so that they may be saved. We as Christians should continually try to teach and practice love in its purest sense and let God work through us as we become more Christ like.

Jesus said, "I am the way and the truth and the life. No one comes to the Father except through me" (John 14:6). What if you used the word *love*? "Love is the way and the truth and the life. No one comes to the Father except through love." Jesus is one with God, and God is love.

"God is love, and whoever abides in love abides in God and God abides in him" (1 John 4:16).

"And I assure you that the time is coming, in fact it is here, when the dead will hear my voice, the voice of the Son of God, and those who listen will live" (John 5:25).

1. In English, we refer to the Supreme Being as God. Is that Supreme Being no less God if we speak another language? French = *Dieu*, Greek = *Thios*, Italian = *Dio*, Arabic = *Allah*.
2. Do you believe that babies who die and are not baptized go to heaven?
3. Noah had never heard of Jesus; did he go to hell? What about Moses?
4. Since Jesus is love, what would be different if we used the word *love* everywhere in scriptures instead of *Jesus*?
5. If you had the power, would you have all of your loved ones in heaven when you are there? Are you more forgiving than God?
6. If we would not let those loved ones who didn't go to church into heaven, are we being less loving? Are we acting like a Pharisee? Are we taking over the role of Jesus to judge the living and the dead?
7. While we all know that scriptures are sometimes confusing, a matter of semantics, should we not try to understand their message from a more inclusive point of view?

Lasting Friendships

Question: Can you remember a story about a friend from your youth? Are you still friends?

Recently, I was called upon to preside over a graveside service for an old friend. I had not seen Sandra Brown or communicated with her for years. This separation by time, space, and circumstance caused me to think about how good a friend I had been to her. Sandra's brother, Armon, had been my best friend coming up, and we remained friends, even though God took him home before his younger sister. It was Armon's widow Andrea who asked me to preside at Sandra's service

I told the assembled friends and family that I was unable to speak about the adult Sandra, but I felt that if I just talked about the Sandra I knew years ago and the family and community that raised her, we would find that it was the same person they knew and loved. Sandra might have been shocked if she was told before she passed that Jimmy Dille would preside over her service. I think for some reason, God wanted it to happen.

I had looked for Sandra's father's gravesite for several years. Mr. Brown had died when Sandra was still in high school. I remember attending his funeral, but I could not remember where he was buried. One day, a few years ago after placing flowers upon my grandparents' grave, I wandered around the old cemetery, remembering the many people from my old hometown who were interred there. I was over in the Catholic section when I felt something leading me back in the direction toward my grandparents' grave. As I approached their site, I was pulled to the back edge of the beautiful sacred resting place of so many, from as long ago as 1870. As I approached the last row of stones, I was wondering what was pulling me

Answers | 111

there. As I read the last stone in the last row, I was somewhat shocked; there was Mr. Armon K. Brown Sr., all alone in the back corner under some ancient cedars. I had an extra flower, so I placed it next to the stone. The next time I visited my grandparents' gravesite, I again placed flowers on Mr. Brown's grave, and there beside his stone was Sandra's. She intended to be interred next to her dad and had already bought her simple stone. Now that day had arrived, and her ashes were placed in that place next to her father, according to her wishes.

I remembered the kindness of Mr. Brown as I spoke to those gathered for Sandra's celebration of life. When I was a young man, he had given me not one but a second "pick of the litter" beagle pup. The first one only lived a few weeks when the school bus ran it over. Mr. Brown sent word by Armon that I could come and pick another. He taught us about hunting skills, and I even have his shotgun to this day. A man's shotgun was something that was prized in the old days; it was usually passed on to his firstborn son. Since Armon already possessed a gun just like his dad's, he traded his dad's gun for mine, which had been a Christmas gift from my parents. The old shotgun is not valuable, but to me, it's a symbol of friendship I still treasure.

When I offered it back to Armon a year before cancer took him, he thought a while and then replied, "No, Jimmy, you need to keep it."

I talked about the people who inhabited our hometown and about Sandra's grandmother, mother, and father. I talked about the character of the family and the character of Sandra, who I knew sixty years ago. I told those in attendance that true friendships never died, even if time and circumstance separate you. I talked about the club Armon and I had formed years ago, pledging that it would never die, like the other clubs we created had. We haven't had a meeting for a while, I said, but we had one planned under an ancient beech tree in a heavenly place.

Over these many years and many friendships I've been blessed with, I've noticed the requirements are always the same. There must first be trust and tolerance, then common interests and pursuits. Trust is the first thing required for any loving relationship. Without trust, there can be no lasting bond. Common interests may appear to be a sport, such as hunting or baseball; however, it really is a common understanding of what love is. Love is something God desires each of us to understand; it's the true purpose of our life here on earth. Love that is shared is a strong bond that will be difficult (if not impossible) to break. Just as the love between our God and us, it can only be broken if we deny it. True friendship requires tending. Like a garden left untended, relationships will wither if we do not tend to them. If you are a friend, you will make regular contact to update and be updated. Phones ring both ways; we cannot be a friend if we don't check in occasionally. You cannot stay in your corner of the world, waiting for friends to come to you; occasionally, you have to go to them. Don't complain that your children never call you if you never call them.

There is one friend who will always be there for us, even if we fail to check in regularly. That friend is Jesus.

"I have loved you even as the Father has loved me. Remain in my love. When you obey me, you remain in my love, just as I obey my Father and remain in his love. I have told you this so that you will be filled with my joy. Yes, your joy will overflow! I command you to love each other in the same way that I love you. And here is how to measure it—the greatest love is shown when people lay down their lives for their friends. You are my friends if you obey me. I no longer call you servants, because a master doesn't confide in his servants. Now you are my friends, since I have told you everything the Father told me. You didn't choose me. I chose you. I appointed you to go and produce fruit that will last, so that the Father will give you whatever you ask for using my name. I command you to love each other" (John 15:9–17).

1. Do you call your friends and family regularly?
2. Do you call your God regularly in prayer?
3. Are you quick to forgive a friend who makes a mistake?
4. Do you find it difficult to trust people?

5. Which of your friends would you like to give the eulogy at your funeral?

"Trust is the glue of life. It's the most essential ingredient in effective communication. It's the foundational principle that holds all relationships."—Stephen Covey

Leadership

Question: Have you ever been pushed into a position of leadership which you didn't want or think you were suited for?

One Monday morning, I was in a conversation with my son about the Mondays of life and how we all feel pressure to get everything done on Monday. I told him that if he did succeed in getting it all done, then what would his employees do? I was reminded of the scene in the movie *Forrest Gump*, when Forrest was jogging across the country, gathering followers along the way. Forrest finally stopped and said, "I'm tired. I think I will go home now." His followers all of a sudden looked perplexed, as if to say, "I've been following this guy, thinking we were all into something wonderful that would soon be discovered, when he just stops before reaching some mystical goal; now what are we going to do?"

Sometimes, we seem to be following someone who's leading us to nowhere in this life. Sometimes, we put all of our faith into other people, making them our leaders, without fully understanding where we are going. There was another old movie, *Being There*, which followed the same theme. Peter Sellers plays a dimwitted gardener of a wealthy man, who wanders off after his boss dies. He soon is involved in events that make others think he is brilliant, so they make him their leader. He became Chance Gardener and was on his way to becoming president of the United States, with no plan of his own.

Leadership roles are sometimes thrust upon us, even though we may not be equipped to be in that role. Some people grow into their leadership roles, and others languish, leaving their followers frustrated. Leaders who are successful are often not recognized until much later. I think Harry

Truman is a good example. Truman had little formal education, but events placed him as leader of our country during a tumultuous period of war, racism, and economic uncertainty. Truman made difficult decisions that I think saved the country and other parts of the world from more disaster and hatred, including the using the atom bomb, developing the Marshall Plan, integrating the military, and standing up to communism

Christians believe that the greatest leader in this universe is Jesus and if we follow his example, we will have a full, happy life here and an eternal life with him after we leave this world. It's a fatal mistake to put our faith in those who want us to believe if we follow them, we will have utopia here on earth.

If we live our life following false teachers, we will seek to be a prince or a princess. We will want others to serve us instead of serving others. We will want others to forgive our transgressions but not forgive them theirs. If we look for faults instead of goodness in others, we will find them, thereby making our own lives unhappy. If Jesus looked for faults instead of goodness in his apostles, he would never have chosen any of them to fill the roles thrust upon them.

We Christians should accept our leadership roles and quit asking others to serve us. We are not princes or princesses but rooted in Christ to become leaders. We will not solve all the world's ills and fix every broken person on one Monday, but we can begin by fixing ourselves, and then we can begin to change the world by our example. They will know us by our love. Although people have different gifts, love is available to everyone. Our philosophy should be as the Prayer of St. Francis describes:

The Prayer of St. Francis

Lord, make me an instrument of your peace.
Where there is hatred, let me sow love.
Where there is injury, pardon.
Where there is doubt, faith.
Where there is despair, hope.
Where there is darkness, light.

O Divine Master, grant that I may not so much seek to be consoled as to console.

To be understood as to understand.
To be loved as to love.
For it is in giving that we receive.
It is in pardoning that we are pardoned.
And it is dying that we are born to eternal life.

"If I could speak in any language in heaven or earth but didn't love others I would only be making meaningless noise like a loud gong or a clanging cymbal. If I had the gift of prophecy, and knew all the mysteries of the future and knew everything about everything, but didn't love others, what good would I be? And if I had the gift of faith so that I could speak to a mountain and make it move, without love I would be no good to anybody. If I gave everything I have to the poor and even sacrificed my body, I could boast about it, but if I didn't love others, I would be of no value whatsoever.

"Love is patient and kind. Love is not jealous or boastful or proud or rude. Love does not demand its own way. Love is not irritable, and it keeps no record of when it has been wronged. It is never glad about injustice but rejoices whenever the truth wins out. Love never gives up, never loses faith, is always hopeful and endures through every circumstance" (1 Corinthians 13:1–13).

1. Do you ever gossip about the faults or shortcomings of others?
2. Are you ever jealous of someone's gifts and talents?
3. Do you always feel the need to get it all done on Monday?
4. Did anyone you were following just quit, making you quit also?
5. Have you ever said, "This preacher just doesn't inspire me," instead of trying to inspire him?
6. Do you ever try to understand why others behave in ways you disagree with?

"I'm not a smart man, but I know what love is."—Forrest Gump

"As long as the roots are not severed, all is well, and all will be well in the garden."—Chance Gardener

Listen to the Music

Question: When was the last time you stepped outside and really appreciated the sounds, smells, and beauty of earth? Can you describe one of those occasions?

I recently listened to an interview of an astronaut who had spent months aboard the International Space Station. The question that most intrigued me was, "What was the biggest psychological problem you had to deal with while spending that much time in space?" The astronaut thought for a second then said, "I missed earth." The interview was taking place outside, and the astronaut said, "Listen to that bird singing; listen to the wind whispering through the trees. You do not hear those sounds in space." It made me think of a book a physician wrote about his near-death experience. He said that in his view of heaven, there was music so enthralling that you were completely conscious of it emanating from everything; even the trees and grass produced this beautiful music. I have since thought that we become so accustomed to the beauty of nature, we ignore it. Our minds are usually focused upon the task at hand that is necessary in order to survive physically; however, at times, we need to focus upon the music the earth makes and the beauty it produces visually. We have to do this in order to maintain our God-given spirit. I sometimes think children do a better job of appreciating earth than adults do. Have you ever watched small children playing? They will instantly find a little flower to pick or notice the sound of a bird singing in a tree. They are more in tune with nature because they have not been living in it long enough to become unconscious of its beauty and presence. We soon learn to sense those things that might harm us and react in a way that will protect us from danger; this is necessary, but somehow, we fail to keep that sense of wonder that a child has with our environment. That old saying "Stop and smell the roses" rings true when we get so focused on seeking wealth and power in this beautiful world, we fail to appreciate the important things about life and our earth.

April 22 was designated as Earth Day, and although I didn't approve of some celebrants I saw on TV, I believe that we are placed on this earth to learn to love. Our purpose is to learn and maintain love of God, self, other people, and our earth with its creatures and resources. Protection of the plants and animals that God has surrounded us with is part of learning about love. Unfortunately, some people become so zealous about protecting everything that they forget that we must survive. Survive because we are made in the image of God. Environmental zealots want to protect everything to the point they often fail to understand that God gave us plants and animals so that humans could survive. If you have watched any of the popular survival shows on TV, you will notice that even the most enthusiastic environmentalists will learn they need to use the plants and animals to survive.

All this may seem so fundamental that you may say, "Well, everyone understands this." I am sure this is true in varying degrees; however, I believe God wants us to refresh our primeval appreciation of his gift of life. We should help others see the beauty of our world that exists in spite of our misuse and its ever-present dangers. My pastor this past Sunday told us to find those negative thoughts in our mind and replace them with positive thoughts. Good advice to follow in our long trip back home.

"Then God looked over all he had made, and he saw that it was excellent in every way. That all happened on the sixth day" (Genesis 1:31).

1. Do you see windows as things that need to be cleaned or as things that allow us to see the beauty of the world?
2. Do you sometimes let problems fill your mind to the point you cannot see opportunity?
3. Helen Keller could not hear or see, yet she learned to understand love. Do you sometimes fail to use all your God-given senses?
4. Who in your life helped you appreciate the beauty that surrounds all of us?

5. Did you see the recent video of a man born color blind who put on glasses that helped him to see the world in color? Did you cry with him a little?
6. Most of the astronauts saw the delicate beauty of our earth from far away and appreciated it. Why do we have to be far removed from some things before we can really appreciate them?

"The earth has music for those who listen."—George Santayana

"We came all this way to explore the moon, and the most important thing is that we discovered the earth."—William Anders, Apollo astronaut

Mother Earth Day produces a few nuts, but without a few nuts, we would not have trees.

Beauty is in the ideal of perfect harmony
Which is in the universal being;
Truth the perfect comprehension of the universal mind.
Rabindranath Tagore

I died for beauty, but was scarce
Adjusted in the tomb,
When one who died for truth was lain
In an adjoining room.

He questioned softly why I failed?
"For beauty," I replied.
"And I for truth, -the two are one;
We brethren are," he said.

And so, as kinsmen met a night,
We talked between the rooms,
Until the moss had reached our lips,
And covered up our names.
Emily Dickinson

Love-Hate (Two Sides of the Same Issue)

Question: Is it possible to be equally on both sides of an issue? Can you think of an issue that you believe has compelling arguments on both sides?

In the George Orwell novel *1984*, the thought police convince people that black is white and, furthermore, they never had thought otherwise. Politicians today have the ability to convince people in the real world that some things happened differently in the past than we think, thus creating a new reality in our minds. We are told by psychologists that it is possible to have a love-hate relationship because of the many facets of what seem to be opposite concepts. Hate has many aspects and love even more; therefore, it can be logically possible to love someone and hate them at the same time. We may love some aspects but hate other traits of an individual. It seems the same in legislation, where some parts of a bill are fine in our mind, but other parts go against certain values we hold. Often changes proposed to the voters are purposely worded to make us think that black is white, because if written plainly, the voters would not approve.

We sometimes hear people say that they love someone but they don't like them. I think what they are saying is that they love an individual but disapprove of their behavior. All of us behave at times in a manner that creates disharmony enough for disapproval.

We have what seem to be race-related disruptions, which often become violent because certain interests have the ability to convince news media and the masses that left is right and up is really down. This creates emotions that can be manipulated into movements for social change. The people who are affected often do not understand that they are being manipulated by individuals or groups that have an agenda. Our country has sometimes been led into war by similar methods. We also have been led to believe that certain things happened differently than actuality, after wars began or ended, in order to gain some political advantages. Misinformation is a tool used effectively to create emotional responses and create hatred. During World War II, cartoons made us learn to hate Japanese and Germans. Immediately after the war, we were led in an effective way to love them.

I have thought about the core reason for disharmony between individuals, political parties, churches, governments, and nations. There are cultural differences in this world that have developed, sometimes naturally and at other times because of actions by individuals, groups, and even governments. People seek power to feed some primal need, but some seek power in order to promote harmony and a better life for all. Leaders can motivate people to become better educated and better informed so they can provide for themselves and others. Contrarily, leaders can be selfish and mislead people toward a destructive end. I believe the basic reason for hatred is ignorance. At the individual level, we usually lack knowledge when two sides are at conflict. It is the same when cultures clash and nations go to war. If it were possible to gain complete knowledge of situations and actions from both sides of any disagreement, there would be more harmony and less hatred. Unfortunately, there is also something called evil that exists in our world that no amount of information would subdue.

One day, I had a problem arise because of human and computer error. I could have become angry and demanded a just resolution, but I chose to become better informed to get the best answers in order to resolve the problem. I soon discovered that I had been partially responsible, which was why the computer was treating me so inhumanely. I avoided the dispiriting effects of anger by being patient, kind, and tolerant of the person trying to solve my problem, and my morning was kept pleasant, with the problem being solved. I believe that most of the time, we get angry at companies and institutions because we lack understanding. The world would be a better place if we took the time to become better informed before turned angry. Better informed people listen and study all sides of events and conflicts.

Unfortunately, we usually only listen to information presented from a biased point of view, which builds upon our personal bias.

Most of the time when customers at my pharmacy become angry, it is because they are ill-informed about their insurance, their physician's instructions, or government restrictions. Many patients are ignorant of the costly process of developing new medicines through the FDA maze and government bureaucracy. Beginning with the Estes Kefauver hearings sixty years ago, the public has been fed a constant message that the very pharmaceutical company that discovered life-saving medicine is really a greedy company that only wants to make a profit. The government, which wants to control pharmaceutical companies, has not discovered any medicines that I can recall. Many times, patients or their caretakers already have a mind-set that will not allow them to hear facts and receive help. I am afraid that I have been guilty at times of having my mind made up and fail to become better informed about personal, social, political, or religious issues. Sometimes, when I become better informed, I discover that I really agree with the other point of view

Satan's work is fueled by brains that are defective and functioning brains that are ignorant of truths. It should be the greatest goal of Christianity to spread truth and knowledge in a world filled with the holes of ignorance. The love of Christ needs an atmosphere of desire for truth in order to fill those holes, whether they be in personal lives or cultures around the world.

Jesus came into this world to spread the truth of God's love and was crucified by ignorant and misinformed people. He utilized the Jewish faith to show us that we can often be shown that we are arguing about something that we really agree upon, if we only had the knowledge that Christ Jesus came to fulfill the law. We should elevate our thoughts beyond this human existence.

"Under the old system, the blood of goats and bulls and the ashes of a young cow could cleanse people's bodies from ritual defilement. Just think how much more the blood of Christ will purify our hearts from deeds that lead to death so that we can worship the living God. For by the power of the eternal Spirit, Christ offered himself to God as a perfect sacrifice for our sins" (Hebrews 9:13–14).

1. Have you ever debated an issue and won the battle but lost the war because you were thinking at different levels?
2. Jesus did not come to do away with the Jewish faith but to elevate it. Did he love the Jewish faith but disliked how people were interpreting the law?
3. When Jesus said that "the only way to the Father is through me," was he wanting us to think at a higher level? If Jesus is love as he says he is, then was he saying that the only way to the Father is through love? Has love always existed in humankind?
4. When we argue about the sacrament of baptism, whether to dip, sprinkle, or immerse, are we failing to see the elevated view that this is only a symbol of a higher truth?

Mary Mother of Jesus

Question: Have you ever prayed or talked to anyone you think may be in heaven, your mother or father or perhaps a child?

I have stood at the grave of many loved ones and talked to them. Some may think that I was just talking to myself; however, I am not alone in that practice. In Paul's letter to the Corinthians, he says, "If one part suffers, all parts suffer with it."(1 Corinthians 12:26) He was telling us that we are all brothers and sisters in Christ and each of us has a mission, none being less important to the Body of Christ (the church). Saints are sometimes referred to in our Bible as those who have accepted Christ. Saints also are referred to as those who are with God. We are all one; if one suffers, we all suffer. We are told that the greatest commandment is to love our God with all our hearts, all our minds, and all our souls. We are also told that to love each other as we love ourselves is a commandment of equal importance. All other commandments are based upon these two. We are all connected, both the living and the dead, to our loving God. It does not seem too foolish to ask our fellow saints to lift up our voices together, both the living and the dead.

People are often offended by the Roman Catholic practice of honoring Mary the Mother of Jesus and asking her to pray with us. This is confused with the idea that they may be worshiping Mary. Our Father in heaven honored Mary in the most important way, by bringing his own being into our world in the human form of Jesus through her. I believe that if I can talk to my own mother at her grave, telling her how much I appreciate all she did for me, it should be acceptable to talk to Mary, who is blessed among women in the same manner, asking that they both pray with me. For whatever reason, God wants all of us to pray together (Mathew

18:18–20). These words from Jesus seem to tell us that we become more connected to heaven and the Father when we agree on things on earth that are in harmony with our Father. We have a connection with heaven and those who have gone to be with God in heaven.

"Prayer is a very powerful thing; it has parted great waters, and we are told that it can move mountains. Just as our efforts to please our Father by singing together, we are encouraged to pray together. Both of these exercises please our Father because we become more in harmony as we hear and feel our beloved brothers and sisters harmonizing with our praise and prayers' (Romans 8:28).

How many of us knew we could approach our earthly father anytime but we sought comfort from our mother to go to him to ask him to favor us in some way? Is it unreasonable to beseech, Mary, the one chosen to be the mother of his only son, to pray to God the Father with us?

We Christians recite the Apostle's Creed during services and often fail to listen to our own words. We say that we believe in the communion of saints, which means that we believe we are connected to each other as well as the saints in heaven. Are we forbidden to ask them to pray with us?

"Elizabeth gave a glad cry and exclaimed to Mary, 'You are blessed by God above all other women, and your child is blessed. What an honor this is, that the mother of my Lord should visit me! When you came in and greeted me, my baby jumped for joy the instant I heard your voice! You are blessed, because you believed that the Lord would do what he said'" (Luke 1:42–45).

The Hail Mary prayer is based upon this scripture.

"Hail Mary, full of grace, the Lord is with you. Blessed art thou among women and blessed is the fruit of thy womb, Jesus. Holy Mary, mother of God, pray for us sinners now and at the hour of our death. Amen."

1. If our scriptures tell us that Mary was blessed among women, is it because she was found to be in special favor with God?

2. If God knows our needs and also what we deserve, why bother to pray?
3. Have you ever asked your friends to pray with you, asking God to heal a loved one? Why not just pray yourself?
4. Does it do any harm to ask saints to pray with us?
5. Would you dishonor God by asking me to pray with you?
6. Do you feel honored when someone compliments you? Do you feel more honored if many people compliment you?

I once sang a song poorly but was joined by someone who harmonized, and my song gained beauty.

Miracles Unrecognized

Question: Can you think of something that happened in your life that can only be described as a miracle, large or small?

Miracles may be profound events that defy understanding by the human mind, or they may be very small even unrecognized events in our daily life that defy logic and intellect. We walk past miracles each day of our lives. I sowed grass seed last week and assumed that some of it would germinate and grow, making my lawn more attractive. I gave little thought to the miracle of germination and genetic instructions present in that grass seed. Science can perhaps describe the process and the blueprint. However, science cannot tell us how all the various seeds of nature got their orders to proceed with the process of continuing the miracle of life. The larva that found a leaf and attached itself so that it could develop a cocoon where it could evolve into a butterfly is just taken for granted. What a miracle that process is, if we stop to think about it. We also take for granted the sunlight that illuminates our pathway, which contains energy that stimulates all growth, not stopping to ponder what a miracle this ray of sunshine really is.

What a miracles really is, is God, the source of all energy and love, present all around us and in us at every moment of our lives. We are only given limited ability to understand all things great and small, but we should utilize this limited ability to understand and worship the source of everything visible and invisible. There are things we need to focus upon in order to live in God's universe; we need to work to provide food and shelter, but we need to be in a constant state of awareness of the presence of God in three persons. We need to understand that to be a Christian, we have to love others and our environment. We need to give credit for these miracles to our Lord by learning to love in the manner taught by Jesus.

Sometimes, our Lord provides gifts in a form that can only be described as a miracle. We often let even these gifts go unrecognized and unappreciated. I have personally been the recipient of God's favor of miracles and sometimes try to give credit to science or accidental coincidence. I have to constantly remind myself to ignore the methods of Satan's pleadings. A few years ago, my ophthalmologist examined my eyes and informed me that I had macular degeneration. I also had cataracts developing in both eyes. The doctor said this was happening because the rods and cones in my eyes were breaking down, leaving fatty deposits called drusen behind my macula. This process was in the dry stage but would probably proceed to what they call the wet kind. At the wet stage, I probably would lose my center vision completely, leaving only peripheral vision. I eventually had cataract surgery, which disappointingly did not improve my vision much. I prayed and had faith that I could accept my fate if I was to be partially blind, but I also asked for a miracle.

A few months ago, my doctor said that the "bubbles" under my macula were to the point that they would likely begin to break, in simple terms. The results would be loss of sight. He said that upon my return visit, he could give me injections in my eyes that would slow the process somewhat. When I returned, they took pictures of my retina and compared them with past pictures. Upon examination, the doctor seemed to be a little perplexed, saying that something strange had happened.

"Do you see this disruption of your macula in the older pictures?" he asked. "Well, look at these pictures today. The macula has smoothed out."

I had noticed that my vision was improving; I didn't even need glasses to read most of the time. Upon utilizing the eye charts, I was informed that my vision had indeed improved. The next visit, I saw a new ophthalmologist, who took a lot of time explaining what had happened. I asked her how often this happens.

She responded, "Not very often. In fact, never."

When I told my friends about this miraculous improvement, they sometimes act as if they believe me; however, it's apparent that they really think there must be another explanation other than an act of God. They probably think, *Why would God give this sinner such a miracle?* I sometimes even think the same thing. I have to go through the whole process in my mind, and I can only attribute this to a miracle of God. My task has to be to attribute and utilize this gifted miracle to the glory of God, who provided it. I understand that I must appreciate my newfound vision and be about God's work as best I can.

I now understand that God sometimes has to get our attention by unpleasant means so that we will do his work in this wonderful world. We must recognize miracles, large and small, and use the faith they provide to glorify God.

I have a fear that I may sometime in the future fail to live up to the gift I have received and lose my eyesight again. I understand that I must be vigilant in listening to God and his desires for my obedience. I must see the miracles around me every day and thank the Lord for them. I must avoid sin.

"Afterward Jesus returned to Jerusalem for one of the Jewish holy days. Inside the city, near the Sheep Gate, was the pool of Bethesda, with five covered porches. Crowds of sick people—blind, lame or paralyzed—lay on the porches. One of the men lying there had been sick for thirty-eight years. When Jesus saw him and knew how long he had been ill, he asked him, 'Would you like to get well?'

"'I can't sir,' the sick man said. 'I have no one to help me into the pool when the water is stirred up. While I am trying to get there, someone else always gets in ahead of me.' Jesus told him, 'Stand up pickup your sleeping mat, and walk!'

"Instantly, the man was healed! He rolled up the mat and began walking! But this miracle happened on the Sabbath day. So the Jewish leaders objected. They said to the man who was cured, 'You can't work on the Sabbath! It's illegal to carry that sleeping mat!' He replied, 'The man who healed me said to me, "Pick up your sleeping mat and walk."'

"'Who said such a thing as that?' they demanded.

"The man didn't know, for Jesus had disappeared into the crowd. But afterward Jesus found him in the Temple and told him, 'Now you are well; so stop sinning, or something even worse may happen to you.' Then the man went to find the Jewish leaders and told them it was Jesus who had healed him" (John 5:1–17).

1. Have you ever failed to give God the credit he deserves?
2. Is it sin to fail to give our Lord credit for miracles?
3. Do you want to find an explanation other than God for miracles?
4. Do you care for the miracle of nature by preserving natural things and not abusing these gifts?
5. Is the act of doing harm to our environment a sin against God?

Moral Wisdom

Question: Do you ever think about the process that goes on in your own mind when making moral decisions? Do you think you can change that process? How can you change it?

There is much in the news about morality because of the recent political campaign, each side accusing the other of poor moral judgments, lying, vulgar language, and other bad moral behavior. This probably tends to make most people a little uncomfortable because it reminds them of some of their own moral misjudgments. The question we should be trying to understand is, how do we make these moral choices; by what method do we arrive at a decision of any kind, and do we use that same pathway in every decision including moral decisions? Should we as individuals be more concerned with what is moral or immoral, or with how we decide what is moral or immoral? To make moral progress, we need to understand our own thought processes in order to improve the end results, or we will be giving up control of our own individual will. If we understand the unconscious biases and thought processes that influence our moral decision-making, we're better equipped to decide if we're reaching our decisions in a valid way.

We Christians believe that we should begin any decision from the basis of understanding that we have the spirit of God living within each of us. That should be the starting point of our thought processes. Without God at the center of our being, we tend to follow that personality component that wants to satisfy our most basic urges or need for pleasure or comfort, which Freud called our id.

As we grow as Christians, we can only make moral progress if we become more conscious of where we are starting when we begin those thought processes that end with action or some behavior. I overheard a discussion recently concerning the morality or immorality of abortion. I was encouraged as a Christian to hear one man take a stand condemning abortion in spite of the current political correctness. He was explaining that he was beginning his thought process by believing that a human received a soul from God at the time of conception and therefore life had begun. The other person was beginning his thought process from a point of convenience for the mother. We may differ in our opinion of the right or wrongness of their moral judgments, but it seemed that the anti-abortion thought was coming from the starting point of understanding our connection to a God. The pro-abortion thought process was only thinking from that Freudian personality component, the id.

Christianity teaches us that we are born with an evil nature (perhaps this is the id Freud talked about) and can only overcome this by accepting Christ and availing ourselves of God's special favor. The beginning of the understanding of this gives us a thought process that will be in the direction of good moral judgments and decisions. The information we seek and absorb will feed our evil nature or our Christlike nature. We may not even be seeking information that will influence our moral thought processes, but it may be being fed to us in a subliminal method by those who want to control our way of thinking. Christians should utilize the light of Christ to help us discern the basis and biases of information before we internalize it and let it influence our decision-making.

"Once you were dead, doomed forever because of your many sins. You used to live just like the rest of the world, full of sin, obeying Satan, the mighty prince of power of the air. He is the spirit at work in the hearts of those who refuse to obey God. All of us used to live that way, following the passions and desires of our evil nature. We were born with an evil nature, and we were under God's anger just like everyone else.

"But God is so rich in mercy and he loved us so very much. That even while we were dead because of our sins, he gave us life when he raised Christ from the dead. (It is only by God's special favor that you have been saved!) For he raised us from the dead along with Christ, and we are seated with him in the heavenly realms—all because we are one with Christ Jesus. And so God can always point to us as examples of the incredible wealth of his favor and kindness toward us, as shown in all he has done for us through Christ Jesus" (Ephesians 2:1–7).

1. Do you begin making all decisions from the Christ within you?
2. Should we as Christians want our leaders making their decisions based upon an understanding of Christ within them?
3. Have you ever allowed evil or immoral thoughts influence your behavior?
4. What president of the United States do you think most often made decisions based upon Christian principles?
5. Do you believe our children are being taught to understand their thought processes? Are they being taught how to think or just what to think?
6. Do you take quiet time out each day to think about how you think?

Oldtown USA

Question: If you could create a town, what would it be like?

I read about a developer near Atlanta who is creating new communities that are like towns back in the thirties or forties. I have often thought that this would be great if I had the means to create a new town; I have a few ideas. I would find an area near a river and railroad that would be nestled in a valley. I would lay out the streets expanding from a central downtown. The streets would all be lined with sidewalks, and the original trees would be preserved. I would have merchants in the downtown, as they were before shopping centers. There would be grocery stores, hardware stores, ladies' shops, and men's stores. A sporting goods store would be needed to supply the schools, and a couple of barber shops and beauty shops to make us pretty and to gain wisdom and gossip of the day. Maybe a local car dealer or two and a locally owned hospital would be necessary. There would be a couple churches on hills at each end of town. Everything would be within walking distance, and walking would be encouraged. All homes would have front porches and nice lawns. The schools would be locally controlled, and prayer would be required each day, along with the Pledge of Allegiance before classes started.

My wife discouraged me by saying that Walmart would build a huge store near the town, taking all the business from the local merchants. The EPA would file suit because of the snail darter being decimated by the runoff from the new constriction. We would have to defend a suit from some government agency for lack of diversity. Our hospital would have to close because it didn't meet the standards of Obamacare, and our physician would be shunned because he required payment of services from all patients, and they would be required to bill their own insurance company. The town water supply would be shut down by a federal agency because the natural fluoride level is too high. Then of course the schools would be closed because of mentioning God. Our citizens would soon go to larger cities for supplies because they would think the local merchants' prices were too high. We would start to accept federal money, giving up control of our town to the federal government and its regulations.

If we could solve all these problems and create an idyllic little community, how long would it be before the second-generation residents would become slovenly and not care about our original plans and park their trucks on the sidewalks and their RVs in the front lawn? Some might begin to steal from others and vandalize property. Then we would have to build a jail. We would be back to the same situation we have in our towns now. Planned cities like Washington DC and Brasilia, the capital of Brazil, both deteriorated from the original plans.

There was a time when people had God in their lives, pride in their homes, and pride in being clean and neatly dressed. There was a time in America when families seldom missed church on Sundays and loved their neighbors. We even visited with our neighbors as they walked past our front porches. There was a time when we ran our schools locally and trusted our local physician completely. We even billed our own insurance companies. Sadly, there are soon-to-be citizens who don't remember what we used to be and don't have much respect for authority; they want the government to take care of most of their needs. Their God will be somewhere behind a bureaucratic maze, like the Wizard of Oz.

What is it that dreamers really want? I think it is to return to a simpler time when we communicated better personally and had more respect for each other and God's world. Just because we create a new town doesn't mean we can demand people to be Christians and live Christian lives. God has given us freedom to live our lives to serve him or serve ourselves. We are placed in this imperfect world to see contrasts between good and evil and to choose our own path. God wants us to follow a path that is filled with love and, in the process, love each other and our Lord. It seems so simple, but the temptation to live a selfish life is strong. We want what we want now, and sometimes, we want what is not ours to take.

That beautiful town we think we can create would be filled with imperfect people who sometimes make wrong choices that lead to bad results. Learning about God's will and following God's will often requires hard work and self-discipline. We learn these values from our parents and other teachers if we will only listen. As adults, we need to continue to listen to the Spirit of God that dwells within each of us. We hopefully learn to provide for ourselves but help those in need. We need to learn to love ourselves first. The "you" that God created is unique and wonderful. Then we can love others in the way our Lord instructs us to do. This is how we love our Lord and the universe he created.

"As the boys grew up, Esau became a skillful hunter, a man of the open fields, while Jacob was the kind of person who liked to stay at home. Isaac loved Esau in particular because of the wild game he brought home. But Rebekah favored Jacob.

"One day when Jacob was cooking some stew, Esau arrived home exhausted and hungry from a hunt. Esau said to Jacob, 'I'm starved! Give me some of that red stew you've made.' (This was how Esau got his other name, Edam: 'Red.') Jacob replied, 'All right, but trade me your birthright for it.' 'Look, I'm dying of starvation,' said Esau. 'What good is my birthright to me now?' So Jacob insisted. 'Well then, swear to me right now that it is mine.' So Esau swore an oath, thereby selling all his rights as the firstborn to his younger brother. Then Jacob gave Esau some bread and lentil stew. Esau ate and drank and went on about his business, indifferent to the fact that he had given up his birthright" (Genesis 25:27–34).

1. If you could control the people admitted to your imaginary town, would you allow in people who followed Sharia law?
2. Would you have some requirements about people's religion (or lack of religion)?
3. Would you let known criminals come live in your town?

4. Would you let people who were not citizens of your town vote in the elections?
5. Would you accept federal money to help your schools if there were strings and regulations attached?
6. Would you let citizens of your town pass their property on to their children, or would they have to pass a big portion of their estate back to the town?
7. Do you think we sometimes make Jacob's mistake and give up our God-given rights to governing bodies for immediate desires, without pausing to consider the long-range consequences?

Omega

Question: Have you ever moved from a home and felt sentimental about the memories created in that home?

Everything we know in this old world had a beginning, and most have an end of some kind. Our own bodies have a beginning and an end in this world. This world is all we have to relate to in a human sense, and our faith carries the rest.

I have said to all my family that I get sentimental about motel rooms. Sentiment is a driving force in my soul. I see value in places that most people will not attempt to understand, but I would not give up these feelings because I think they are rooted in love. We are placed in this world to discover, understand, and spread love. Jesus said that the two most important things we should do is to love our God and love each other; all the rest of the law is based upon these concepts of our faith. I believe that we cannot just love God and his people without loving the world we abide in. Every event in our lives happens in a particular space and a particular time. We take photos and videos trying to capture these events, but they are cemented into our hearts and minds to view anytime, if we learn about love.

I will always remember that fall day back in 1951, when my brother and I were getting ready to hitchhike home from ball practice. Someone said that our grandparents' house was on fire in Villa Ridge. Somehow, we immediately got a ride the three miles home, only to find the flames had pretty well finished consuming the house we both loved so much. We had experienced so many wonderful times in that old house, we felt that a part of our inner being was going up in flames. The Christmases, Thanksgiving meals, Fourth of July cookouts, and games played inside and out; our hands had touched and explored every inch of that house and formed a permanent attachment that would last a lifetime.

As we ran up the hill past the grade school where we spent eight years, we saw our Grandpa Dille sitting in a lawn chair, with tears streaming down his face. No one was much paying attention to him; I witnessed a similar scene a few years later, when he sat under an awning at his wife's burial. I should have gone up and hugged him each time. Sometimes, just a hand on a shoulder will do.

When my mother moved away from the home we had grown up in, I had tears in my eyes. My dad had been gone a few years, and after Mom remarried, they stayed a few more years and then decided to sell and move to a larger town, thirty-five miles away. The feelings I had for this old two-story house were even stronger than those I had for my grandparents' house; both had been filled with love for many years. I walked through the almost empty house that day and went out the back door, not knowing that I wouldn't reenter that sacred place until some forty years later, when it was empty and in disrepair. When my brother and I had the opportunity to go through that old empty house that day, we were flooded with memories and emotions. We could see events in the past like a play unfolding on a stage. So many people gone, so many wonderful times, so many tears.

Some fifty or so years ago, my young wife and I walked through the door of a home that was just framework, a framework within which to build many lives. We had many dreams for this home we had just purchased. It was our first home to own and build memories within. Our three small girls would be given the gift of a wonderful little brother within a year. A couple years later, they also would lose a little brother who never had a chance to live in this world.

Our friends lived in the new house next door, and they had three children. The Ripleys were in so many ways just like us and shared the same values. Rip had just started a medical practice, as I also had just started a career in pharmacy. Life would be good for several years. Hard work, not much money, but lots of love and wonderful friends coming and going. The neighborhood filled with future friends, most of whom are now gone, along with my wife and my life of those years. Things that we didn't really understand made our marriage end. We remained friends, however, and found peace through forgiveness and understanding provided by faith.

This morning, Mary and I went over to say goodbye to my daughter and her husband, as they were preparing to leave for a new home in a city some four hours away. I didn't really think much about it as we drove a few blocks to say goodbye, until I saw the moving van in the driveway. All of a sudden, movies began to play in my mind: the lawn I had laid fifty years ago. This same lawn where I had taught my son to pitch a baseball and watched them all roll in piles of leaves. The front door that I had passed through fifty years ago was a window into the past. The empty house was filled with laughter of friends long gone. My mom and dad were sitting on a couch, waiting for my uncle to come to add central air to our new home. There were old friends laughing somewhere off in the distance. An old black-and-white TV played *I Love Lucy*, and later, there were four little bodies lined up on a rug to watch *The Wizard of Oz*. Birthday wishes were being sung around a kitchen table, and children were fondling packages under a Christmas tree. There were teenage girls streaming through the door, and somewhere in the background was a Christmas carol being sung by Johnny Mathis. The lower patio held so many friends to witness a wedding; some stood in the yard. Across the road in the back was a field full of young boys playing football, and there was a blue and white playhouse shaped like a sailing ship full of giggling kids.

As I came back up the stairs, my son-in-law asked if I had seen anything down there (meaning did we miss loading anything).

I said quietly, "Just memories. Who will take those?"

"All of us," said my loving wife, Mary, as she touched my shoulder and heart.

1. Do you tend to look upon the past with regrets more than fondness?
2. When seeing an old home that may be empty do you ever think about the love that filled it in the past?
3. When looking at old photographs do you smile more often than shed a tear?
4. Do you dislike talking about the past? Have you thought about why it is painful?
5. Do you utilize memories to form a better future?

Our Changing World

Question: Do you think it's best to change with the world as it evolves, or do you think it's better to slowly adapt to social, technological, and moral changes as the world turns?

My older brother and his wife just visited for a few days, and we discussed the value of the cell phones. Their opinion was that they are more of an annoyance than of value. I tried to convince them that my i-Phone is really a personal computer that provides so much information that will make life more enjoyable and make all of us better informed about the past present and even the future. An i-Phone should be thought of as a computer which has a phone app.. Unfortunately, all of my arguments fell upon deaf ears. This morning, my daughter, who lives about five hours away, called on my i-Phone, telling me among other things that she really enjoyed the video I sent of my thirteen-year-old grandson's track meet. As Walker was running the four hundred meter race, I described it like a sports announcer, yelling that Walker was in the lead as they made the far turn. I described the other runners trying to catch up, but Walker held his lead over the finish line, winning as his legs began to wobble. My daughter Dawne said she became emotional viewing the video watching her nephew's triumph.

I said in response, "Yes, I have to get a print made to send to my brother and write a letter to try to describe the emotions, but they will fall short of viewing the video."

I had a contrary view of smartphones last weekend while attending a fundraising dinner. I was trying to have a conversation with a couple of young ladies across the table, but they both used their smart phones to send and receive messages while trying to converse with me. We have not sorted out the good manners involved, including the importance of being unconnected for a period of time for certain events.

It is my belief that God wants us to experience our changing world as much as we can. However, there are certain changes that should be studied slowly and judiciously. Values and moral behavior should be among those things we should be judicious about. We Christians have our scriptures and our church leaders to give us counsel, but we also have our own mind that hopefully has been educated and informed (even, perhaps, by utilizing electronic devices and smartphones). We give much value to the Bible being the Word of God, which I personally also believe. It is also my belief, however, that there are many different interpretations of scriptures. There are many versions of the Bible, and some versions have a few different books as well as different words that may have been translated differently from the original texts. When Jesus cautioned the Pharisees that the person without sin should cast the first stone to kill the lady accused of adultery, he was calling upon his knowledge of Jewish scriptures. Deuteronomy 17:7 says, "The witnesses must throw the first stones, and then all the people will join in. In this way, you will purge all evil from among you." Deuteronomy 17:6–7 also says that more than one witness is necessary before putting someone to death. Jesus clearly interpreted what was thought of a clear scriptural truth in a more liberal and merciful way.

There are cultural changes going on in our time that are difficult to accept by many of us, such as continuing to apply the death penalty for certain offences or eliminating it altogether. We are also currently debating various social aspects of homosexuality. Our scriptures apparently condemn the acts as sinful, but one wonders if Jesus would be more lenient toward what many consider as unnatural acts. Would he consider that perhaps some people have a genetic propensity toward homosexuality? In the time Jesus walked this earth, homosexuals were stoned to death, but most would agree that would be a horrible practice in this time. We've discovered that the death penalty has been wrongly applied too many times in the past, and many people are being proven not guilty today because of our ability to perform DNA testing. Women's rights were lacking in the time of Jesus, and there are scriptural writings to support restrictions upon women's rights. Why do we ignore those today? Can some scriptural guidelines be ignored, while others are accepted?

Jesus would sometimes quote scripture to counter scripture the Pharisees tried to use to condemn him. He didn't ever say that one scripture was wrong he would just indicate that perhaps one should not be so staid and inflexible in their interpretations.

Should we be inflexible in our utilization of scriptures as Christians today when approaching decisions about morality and cultural changes? If we are inflexible will we not be just as cruel as some of the Muslim faith today?

"You who are slaves must accept the authority of your masters. Do whatever they tell you—not only if they are kind and reasonable, but even if they are harsh" (1 Peter 2:18).

"In the same way, you wives must accept the authority of your husbands, even those who refuse to accept the Good News" (1 Peter 3:1).

1. Do you believe our interpretation of some scripture has changed over the years?
2. Do you admire people who are inflexible? Would the world be a better place if we were like them?
3. If slaves accepted the authority of their masters, would they not always be slaves?
4. If women always accepted the authority of their husbands, could children be harmed? Should women accept abusive husbands?
5. Do you think technology can make a life more productive and happier?
6. Why do we resist change as we get older? Don't you admire older people who adapt to change?
7. Should women still be required to go outside the city when they have their period?

8. As we become better informed, should we use that information to adjust our moral code?
9. Why do we accept some of the Old Testament rules but not others?
10. If some rules were for those times only, how do we know what rules are for all times?

Please Validate Me

Question: What award did you receive in your life that made you feel good about your accomplishments?

When I was in high school, I was voted most popular, was named captain of our basketball team, and got a trophy as the most valuable player for the softball team. These awards had both positive and negative effects. They made my head swell a little, but they also gave me a little more confidence. Awards have their place, and we must think it is good to validate certain accomplishments and show appreciation for certain skills and behaviors. We give our children certificates, ribbons, stars, and other symbols of validation for sports, Sunday school attendance, and contests. I am reminded of the movie *The Wizard of Oz*, which was about the need for validation. The Scarecrow got a diploma to show he had brains, the Tin Man got a heart, and the Cowardly Lion got a medal for bravery. Soldiers are often awarded the Congressional Medal of Honor. This is our nation's highest award for bravery. We always seem to want validation.

A marriage license is in essence a validation of commitment between husband and wife, even if it gets lost somewhere in the bottom of a dresser. The real validation, however, comes when people understand each other's needs and desires. If a husband or a wife does not respond to a spouse's emotional needs, they may feel unloved and invalidated. The same extends to sexual needs. A husband who does not get response from his wife may not feel validated. The same would be true if a wife does not feel her husband is interested in her needs or desires. When the husband fails to notice her new hairdo or the wonderful meal she worked so hard to prepare, she can feel unloved or invalidated. The relationship established between husband and wife validates their manhood and womanhood. Sometimes, this does not happen, and they are drawn apart.

I once had a boss that had difficulty praising me but found it quite easy to criticize me in front of others. As a young man, I needed to feel appreciated. I needed validation. I learned from him how not to be as a manager of personnel. People make better employees when they get a pat on the back and feel appreciated. I notice that many businesses have an employee of the month award and give the winner a certificate as well as a bonus. I sometimes wonder why anyone was chosen employee of the month for some company that gives poor service. Have you ever wheeled a loved one out of a hospital past these certificates validating employees who didn't keep the place clean or failed to show proper attention to the patients?

I notice that many people have a little Christianity symbol on their bumper; I wonder if this is a good thing or not. If you award yourself this little affirmation of your decision to follow Christ, you better be very careful how you act when someone displeases you with their driving. I know I'm not the best driver now that I have reached senior citizen status, and I guess the lady who passed me that day and waved her middle finger must have agreed. I had a little chuckle when I noticed the little fish on her rear bumper.

Validation is good at various times in our life when others offer it, but we should endeavor to seek real validation from God. We don't need a certificate for a decision to make the love of God and others our driving force. God validates that kind of life with his grace and the promise of everlasting life. There is no better feeling than the confidence when you know you have God in your heart and treat others as you would wish to be treated. God wants us to not seek to be loved but to love. Perhaps validation comes in the form of the love that returns. Real love, however, asks for nothing in return.

We can receive and present all the symbols of validation for doing things expected by our church and religion; however, it is all hollow and religion without substance if you only appear to have faith without putting it to work in your life. Your job can be empty if you feel you're not producing. Your marriage can be empty if each partner is not giving. Your relationship with God can be fruitless if you only seek symbols of your piety.

When Jesus cursed the fig tree that was fruitless and caused it to wither and die, he was showing that the temple in Jerusalem was impressive at first sight, but all the ceremony and grandeur was meaningless because it was not done to worship God. If you only appear to have faith without putting it to work in your life, you are like a fig tree that withered and died because it bore no fruit. Genuine faith means bearing fruit for Christianity.

"In the morning, as Jesus was returning to Jerusalem, he was hungry, and he noticed a fig tree beside the road. He went over to see if there were any figs on it, but there were only leaves. Then he said to it, 'May you never bear fruit again!' And immediately the fig tree withered up" (Matthew 21:18).

1. Have you ever gone to church and left the parking lot a little angry because a car cut you off?
2. Do you expect your spouse to do things for you that you are unwilling to reciprocate? How about a compliment or a little back rub?
3. Do you appreciate good service and offer thanks and a good tip?
4. Do you sometimes fail to talk to your children or grandchildren about the good things they have done but never fail to point out their shortcomings? How about your husband or wife?
5. Do you ever think certain people should not be participating in your worship service?
6. Have you ever noticed a large ostentatious church that was slowly dying and wondered why?

A license to practice medicine does not make someone a physician.

Pleasing God

Question: Can you name some act that you have performed this week that you believe has pleased God?

I recently had a conversation with a close friend, and the next day, he said something we talked about the previous evening had an important meaning for him. He went through our conversation to remind me, asking if I could recall what I had said. We were discussing if people really lived the lives that they wanted to. I said I thought that many times, people live their life in a manner they think will please their parents, even if their parents had been dead for many years. I talked about a couple people we both knew who were still trying to prove worth to their fathers, who had died years ago. I said that we sometimes fail to give up what we think is our parental role, which resulted in years of criticism of our children's decisions and actions. Sometimes, parents only criticize and never provide praise for a job well done or even a hug with a smile. Children, in an effort to receive some kindness, praise, and even love, live their lives in a fashion they think will achieve this, until it controls them. I told my friend that those of us with children and grandchildren should make an effort to change our behavior and release them from our errant criticism. We should tell them about all the things they've accomplished in their lives that have pleased us and tell them how much we love them.

This brings to mind the question of how we should really be living our lives. The things and achievements we seek, both financial and psychological, should be tailored to provide sustenance for ourselves and our families. However, as Christians, we should all try to learn from lessons taught by parents and teachers that the real person to try to please should be our God.

I don't believe God wants us to reshape our own lives by trying to make those around us act in ways we want. Teaching good behavior to our children and even spouses is pleasing to God; however, I believe God wants us to teach with his love in mind. Constant criticism is not loving; it is more akin to harassment. We can wrongly try to remove some guilt from our own souls by criticizing other's behavior.

Criticism can be done in a positive way and with love, if we practice. A wonderful friend who was brilliant, accomplished, and quite wealthy taught me this lesson. If you were in error, he could put his arm around you figuratively and allow you to find a better way and feel good about yourself. My friend never made you think less of yourself in his presence. Many people want you to feel a little below them; this is an error we often make in raising children. Good teachers in whatever role help us understand the value in working together and provide leadership, offering praise when deserved.

If we live our lives with constant criticism of others' behavior and actions, we'll become unwelcome family members, clients, customers, and church members.

Let us release our families from our demands and criticisms so they can live their lives, just as God has released each of us. God offers us his love and the right to live as we please; however, he recommends we live a life of love and gave us his Son as the greatest teacher.

We sometimes want to criticize other Christians for their beliefs when we should be welcoming all believers to seek God's love according to their own beliefs. What we consider wrong may not be wrong in the eyes of other Christians. Let God sort it out.

I found an old clipping in my desk that was a letter to Dear Ann Landers. The father said that he asked his son to write the most important attributes of a good father. To his surprise, the son (who felt he had been unfairly criticized) returned with the following list. We can all learn from this young man's wisdom. I think this would please God.

1. Listen to both sides of an argument and respect the other person's opinion.
2. Accept the fact that every child doesn't have to be "normal."
3. Don't always judge by actions. Consider the motives behind them.
4. Work to increase strengths in the relationship, as well as improve the weaknesses.
5. Don't be overly protective.
6. Consider the harshness of the punishment as compared with the seriousness of the crime.
7. Recognize that I want to be treated like an adult.
8. Emphasize my good points instead of dwelling on the bad.
9. Don't push a child into doing things he doesn't want to do simply because the father would like to do them himself.
10. Realize not everyone has the same abilities and the same ideas of what's important.

Our Lord offers some advice through Paul in Romans:

"Accept Christians who are weak in faith and don't argue with them about what they think is right or wrong. For instance, one person believes it is all right to eat anything. But another believer who has a sensitive conscience will eat only vegetables. Those who think it is all right to eat anything must not look down on those who won't. And those who won't eat certain foods must not condemn those who do, for God has accepted them. Who are you to condemn God's servants? They are responsible to the Lord, so let him tell them whether they are right or wrong. The Lord's power will help them do as they should" (Romans 14:1–4).

1. Do you need to go to each of your children and release them with love and praise?
2. Do you ever try to control God's actions when you pray? ("Lord, please help me, and here is the way I want you to do it.")
3. When teaching, should we treat anyone with less respect?
4. Have you ever tried to relive your life through a child or grandchild by suggesting they play a sport or take up a certain profession?

5. Do you constantly find things to criticize about people who work for you? How about the places you shop?
6. Do you look for things to criticize instead of things to praise? Has it become a habit?

Political Correctness versus Christian Correctness

Question: Do you believe the cultural standards and values in our town, our state, our nation, and our world are improving, about the same, or declining?

It is difficult today to even discuss such things because these issues have become politicized, and people are on different sides of the political spectrum. If a group is made up of a majority of one side of an issue the minority will usually be less vocal and try to present their opposite views in a polite manner if at all. Politeness may fall by the wayside and anger develop because certain phrases have become politically incorrect. Even groups that are all of the same politics may have people who disagree but are afraid they will viewed as sellouts if they don't agree with the majority. The unfortunate effect of all this is that our Christian standards and values may be becoming eroded by political pressure. One might argue that some of these values need to be changed. Others would say that these values are set by our scriptures and therefore unchangeable.

There have always been zealots and idea-driven people trying to force change in their culture. This can be good or bad. The apostle Paul was considered a nut case in his world and would be, even today. Christians, however, think of him as a zealot for good. Hitler is an example of someone who tried to change the world by appealing to a misconception held by many that Jews were responsible for their financial problems. We can see today that Hitler's movement was evil and wrong. People in his country, however, were confined by Nazi political correctness and were afraid to speak their minds

Some would say that we should continue to be vigorous alarmists, which means we should stand on principle and refuse to bend to passing breezes. Even the Roman Catholic Church (for centuries, the only Christian church), used a dead language, Latin, to avoid cultural changes in meaning of words, in order to keep the message of Christ uncorrupted. Reformation became necessary because the church became influenced by wrong-minded leaders. It took courage for the reformers to speak up against the status quo. They did not let political correctness of the time prevent them from challenging the direction the Christian church was going.

We Christians develop our principles from the teachings of Christ and our scriptures. If we seem to be inflexible, we are accused of being radical fundamentalists. This is a technique used by those who do not want their lifestyle to be limited in any way. There are different groups and ideologies that sometimes come together, using the same political techniques to degrade Christian principles they believe interfere with their agenda. Too many Christians today, Catholic and Protestant, Democrats and Republicans, fail to confront these assaults because they don't want to be accused of intolerance.

The news is full of examples of assaults on Christian principles: same-sex marriage, transgenderism, free sex, racism, abortion, parental discipline, and other issues. We go along with the process because we don't want to appear intolerant or uninformed. The term *political correctness* (PC) to some means using language that is sensitive to certain ethnicities, genders, sexual orientation, physical abilities, and so on. To others, PC in application today has become oversensitivity at the expense of common sense and practicality. Some wonder if PC outlaws enough words and phrases, we may have to go to another language. We even have objective truths now being challenged by those who want subjective truths to really be objective (e.g., I feel black; therefore, I am black. I feel like a woman; therefore, I am a woman).

Politeness should be taught by academia instead of correctness, and the problem will go away. Unfortunately, many in academia use PC to advance an agenda. Each of us should ask ourselves if we agree with the agenda and if it fits with our Christian principles, or if we really disagree with the general agenda and want to stand up for those principles. We should be cautious when we try to nail down with certainty these slippery slopes of social change. However, open-minded debate is necessary for constructive change, uninhibited by political correctness.

In his day, Jesus stood up against the corruption of principles in the face of political opposition and social acceptance of those corrupted principles. At the beginning, most thought he was a revolutionary because he seemed to be asking for changes in principles that had become accepted by the masses. What he really introduced was logical understanding of our God and the true meaning of love. Jesus didn't let PC limit his words; he even used politically incorrect words ("You fools" or "You hypocrites"). We Christians should draw upon his teachings to prevent the decline of the principles defining love. We cannot change social reality by changing language. If we believe someone is in error on a certain doctrine we hold as true, we should not fail to inform them but not unkindly. Paul gives us simple advice in this matter in Colossians 4:5–6:

"Live wisely among those who are not Christians, and make the most of every opportunity. Let your conversation be gracious and effective so that you will have the right answer for everyone."

1. Do you sometimes cling to your political party when they espouse social change you disagree with?
2. Since different cultures approach social issues differently, is it better to have a central controlling agency to usher a universal change in our American culture? Or should more local ideas prevail in different states, for instance? Wasn't that what the Civil War was fought over?
3. This subject requires debate, but do you think PC prevents free debate?
4. Do you think the driving force for cultural redefinitions is an anti-Christian movement in our country?

5. If there had not been a redefinition of what an American citizen is, would African Americans have full citizenship? Did this have to be guided by national government to succeed?
6. Have you ever changed your position on a cultural issue?

Polls

Question: Have you ever participated in a national poll? Do you think all polls are accurate?

Polling seems to be ubiquitous today, although most of us have never been polled. We don't even know how the pollsters function these days, when many people have dropped their land line phones. When we had one, and someone called and began their spiel, most of us quickly hung up. I am only interested in this subject today to help us understand how we are manipulated without our awareness. It is not easy to avoid intrusions into our subconscious, promoting a product or candidate. Those wanting cultural changes can put thoughts in our minds that will accumulate and perhaps make us at least less resistant to new views that can become the norm. *Norm* is a shortened form for *normal behavior*, which sometimes is not even politically correct to consider. In our culture today, there seems to be a movement to dumb down our population in a long process of eliminating our resistance to change. We've allowed our schools to become more and more centrally controlled, which makes it easier to control the curriculum. History has been rewritten in a process of making long-held beliefs disappear into the vapor of ignorance. We have allowed history to be rewritten as if it was unimportant to those affected. Christians should be aware that many of these cultural movements for change are a direct assault upon the most sacred principles taught by Jesus.

I was shopping at a big mart recently, and the item I wanted to purchase was locked in a glass enclosure. After waiting for a period, I finally found a salesperson to unlock the cabinet and retrieve the item I wanted. I asked if people often stole these items, and she responded, "Sure, they will steal anything these days."

I muttered in response, "Whatever happened to the sense of right and wrong?" My answer came to my mind: *It was stolen from us.* There may be many reasons for people stealing without much of a sense of the wrongness of the act. I would offer there is cultural acceptance by many that those who have much, perhaps do not really deserve their gains, and therefore, disadvantaged people have the right to take what they need.

Tolstoy, the famous Russian writer, once said, "Wrong does not cease to be wrong because the majority share in it." It has become too easy to develop our principles by thinking that the majority thinks this way, so it must be right. We've all used the phrase, "Well, all my friends are doing it." That way of thinking can lead us down a dark and lonely road. It is easy to quiet that voice of authority speaking in the recesses of our minds, telling us something is wrong.

It takes a thoughtful, informed mind to stay aware of the attempts to pull us away from our Christian principles on a daily basis. We want to be a part of the crowd, not thought of as an extremist. We don't want to be outside the current new way of thinking. Progressive ideas that appear more tolerant are attractive to many Christians. C. S. Lewis once gave a talk at a university called "The Inner Ring." He said, "I believe that in all men's lives at certain periods, and in many men's lives at all periods between infancy and extreme old age, one of the most dominant elements is the desire to be inside the local Ring and the terror of being left outside."

Tolerance is taught by Jesus, so perhaps we should be more tolerant of newly accepted lifestyles or behaviors. The admonition to forgive others in the same manner they forgive us is even in the prayer Jesus gave us. I think he was saying not to judge others, but he also taught to use good judgment about behaving in a way that dishonors God.

Many times, the majority is right, and after personal consideration of how it fits Christian principles, we should lead the crowd. There have been times in our world that the crowd was being led by a force not of God. It is then we should not fear being outside the mainstream thought and stand up for principles Jesus taught.

"Don't let anyone lead you astray with empty philosophy and high-sounding nonsense that come from human thinking and from the evil powers of this world, and not from Christ. For in Christ the fullness of God lives in a human body, and you are complete through your union with Christ. He is the Lord over every ruler and authority in the universe" (Colossians 2:8–10).

When you stand up for Jesus, you may feel that you are standing alone, but he is always with you.

1. Do you often question your own principles when they are outside the norm?
2. When someone else stood up for something you considered right but out of the norm, did you back them up or remain quiet?
3. Can you think of something that most people accept that you don't?
4. Do you think most polls correctly reflect people's opinions?
5. Can you remember a situation where you were in the minority opinion but later proven right?
6. Do you usually listen to someone's opposing viewpoint? Do you usually consider them wrong and quit listening before you respond?

Problem Solving

Question: Can you remember ever just moving on when someone perhaps a stranger had a problem and appeared to need help? Perhaps you remember making the effort to help someone in need?

One night in St. Louis years ago, I started to walk around a man lying on the sidewalk. It was snowing, and alcoholics often stayed in the park across from the drugstore where I worked. I assumed this was just another drunk who wandered across from Tower Grove Park. and I was in a hurry to get home to study for an exam.

As I walked past the man, he pleaded, "My God, man, please help me."

I went back and discovered he had slipped on the steps to his home and broken his leg. I ran up to Grand Avenue and waved a police car down to get help for the man, a simple deed that could have been disastrous if I had not acted.

Life is a continual series of problems to solve. We begin life by trying to learn how to make our fingers work and get something into our mouths. We try to solve the problem of locomotion from crawling to finally walking. Humans take longer than most animals to solve problems, some of which are instinctive with most animals.

When you were a child, you may remember trying to solve a problem but couldn't get an adult to listen to your problem, much less help you solve it. Maybe your problems were not seen as important to a busy adult; therefore, your pleas were often just ignored. Some of these problems were perhaps trivial, but some were important to you at the moment and may have affected you the rest of your life. I am reminded of young children who were being abused and did not know what to do. They probably didn't even understand what was happening to them. There were perhaps incidents of bullying by a sibling causing daily frustration in a child's life. What seems trivial to an adult can be of the utmost importance to a child.

These problems continue throughout our lives, some important and some more trivial, and our skill at identifying problems and seeking knowledge may never be completely developed. It would be great if children had the maturity and wisdom to solve their own problems; unfortunately, it takes life experience and involved teachers and mentors to help children along. People learn ethics, manners, and morals, which we utilize in problem solving. As we become elderly or disabled, we may have the knowledge and wisdom but lack the physical ability to solve our own problems.

Children often lack the vocabulary to adequately describe their problem; adults often suffer the same disability because of sickness or even just lack of education. Language is our most important tool to communicate, but we seldom make the effort to learn better communication skills. As we age, we often cannot find those words that we once could find easily. Young people have a much smaller vocabulary to utilize to solve problems.

What does this mean to us as Christians in our daily life? I think we can all do a better job for ourselves by using more logic and seeking better communication skills. Our duties as Christians do not end with our own problems, however. On a daily basis, we are presented opportunities to help others. Old and young people are often trying to solve problems that we may be able to help with.

I remember watching a frustrated mother in the grocery store, beating her four-year-old child around her face. The mother had obviously reached her limit of patience, but her solution was to become violent towards a defenseless child. I just walked to the next aisle, feeling bad for the child. I have often thought of that incident and wondered how I could have helped. Perhaps I should have picked the young girl up and asked the distraught mother if I could help while she gathered herself. Maybe I could have helped her pay for her groceries; the lack of money may have been the source of her frustration. In today's litigious world, we have to be careful getting involved with strangers, but to do nothing is probably the worst choice. I may not have contributed much that day to a long-term solution of an abusive mother, but I could have shown the child that she was not alone in a world of angry adults.

A man I once knew sexually abused some of his own grandchildren over many years. I only recently learned of his terrible behavior and found out that people in the family knew this was going on years ago but chose to forgive him and go on with life, resulting in him abusing his great-granddaughter. I assume they did not know that such abusers never get rid of their malicious desires. He has gone on to his judgment now, but the girls are still dealing with these terrible abusive incidents. One had been taking care of her bedridden mother and dad but raised the ire of the other siblings because she was smoking marijuana. I said they perhaps should be lenient for her behavior because of her history of abuse years ago.

Her response was, "Well, we tried to forgive him."

I said forgiveness was one thing but forgetting was something else. If something had been done earlier to separate the abuser from contact with young girls, the great-grandchild would not have been abused.

Helping the helpless is an important function of Christian living. We should use prudence in getting involved of course but to do nothing is the worse choice more often.

"Speak up for those who cannot speak for themselves; ensure justice for those who are perishing. Yes speak up for the poor and helpless, and see that they get justice" (Proverbs 31:8–9).

1. In this modern world, are we better off not getting involved in other's problems?
2. While it is much easier to just pass by others needing help, shouldn't we as Christians risk ourselves when we see injustice or need?

3. It is easier to support someone who has spoken up, but do you find it difficult to be that first spokesman?
4. What is the difference between offering help and butting in to someone else's business?
5. Should we remember to try to smile when offering help to an out-of-control parent?
6. Is it always enough to just notify the authorities and not intervene yourself?

Solitude

Question: Do you ever feel the need for solitude? Where do you go to experience solitude?

We only exist because of love, and God is love. We are here on this earth in this universe to learn what love is and try to live it.

Life is filled with evil, danger, and pain. We can become lost in an abyss of distrust, fear, and hopelessness; however, we have to somehow push past the hurt, utilize the lessons learned, and find that innermost part of each soul. When we are able to find our true selves, we will find it is the part of our being that is God. We have to get past those painful memories that haunt us in order to commune with that God within each of us. We all have had experiences that were painful and linger in the recesses of our brains; some of us let these experiences define how we interpret things today in negative ways and utilize the negative when planning for the future. The question we all should ask ourselves is, do I want to live my life relating every experience to the pain, evil, and misunderstandings of the past? Most will answer no if they are honest. Some of us are so damaged by past events, we expect similar things around every corner and have vowed not to be hurt again. They are suspicious of many people and may see them as someone wanting to do them harm.

There is only one way to connect with our soul, the God within us. We have to find solitude on a regular basis and meditate. Some of us sit and think, while others just sit. Solitude means removing all distractions in our surrounding. This may include cell phones, television, music, or whatever will gain your attention. When we are completely in solitude, we don't think about our favorite sports team. We don't think about what has made us mad recently; we should empty our minds of all distractions and focus upon God. This is not easy in today's world, which is filled with distractions. We are being pulled by so many forces we think we are ignoring, but they all pull us, like the moon pulls the tide. Buddhists utilize a mantra, a repeated sound or word or phrase, to help meditate. Catholics do the same thing when repeating certain prayers over and over. The Hail Mary repeated ten times in each of the five decades of the rosary is not so much because the saint does not hear the prayer but to keep the mind focused on meditation. Some people find the rosary service before a Catholic funeral annoying because they don't understand meditation.

God became man to show us what love is. Jesus was and is the perfect example of love. He was confronted with earthly distractions and evil, just as we are, and he showed us how to live a life of love in spite of the unfairness and pain people face. Our scriptures tell us that Jesus often sought solitude in order to listen to God and pray. He found it necessary to remove himself from distractions in order to commune with the God within him. He went to the wilderness for forty days to pray and meditate before beginning his ministry. On the night before his Crucifixion, he went off alone to pray at least twice, and God answered by saying no to his request to remove this cup from him. The earthly distractions were presented to Jesus by Satan, just as they are presented to each of us, and he prevailed over Satan; he accepted the Father's will. We can do the same if we follow the example of the life of Christ. Sometimes, God just says for us to be strong and have faith, and he will be with us in the difficult times.

"Immediately the Holy Spirit compelled Jesus to go into the wilderness. He was there for forty days being tempted by Satan. He was out among the wild animals and angels took care of him" (Mark 1:12).

"And they came to an olive grove called Gethsemane, and Jesus said, 'Sit here while I go and pray.' He took Peter, James and John with him and he began to be filed with horror and deep distress. He told them, 'My soul is crushed with grief to the point of death. Stay here and watch with me.'

"He went on a little farther and fell face down on the ground. He prayed that, if it were possible, the awful hour awaiting him might pass him by.

'Abba, Father,' he said, 'everything is possible for you. Please take this cup of suffering away from me. Yet I want your will not mine'" (Mark 14:32–36).

1. Do you find solitude to be uncomfortable?
2. Have you ever been on a retreat?
3. How do you feel about the Cistercian monks who take a vow of silence?
4. When Jesus prayed, do you think he did more listening than talking?
5. Can you pray without having a written prayer?

"Be still and know that I am God" (Psalm 46:10).

Stillness

Question: Who's home did all the kids hang out around when you were a kid? Why?

My mother wrote to me my first year in college, saying Dad was having a hard time. She said the neighborhood was too still. I was among the last of a bunch of boys who were always playing ball and making the sounds boys make. One night, I noticed that the sounds I've heard for over thirty years from my deck are no longer there. I listened for a while, and there in the distance, I could just hear the voice of a young child. I wasn't sure; maybe it was a dog. Dad made friends with my old dog Rock after I left home and even let him come into the house. Mom said ol' Rock seemed lonely too.

The Miller boy across the street was always washing his car with the stereo blasting loud rock from the eighties. He lost his father at a young age, but his mother loved him twice as much. That bad curve north of town took him and his young passengers one night as they drove home from a rock concert. I missed that loud music on Saturday afternoons after that. A doctor and his young wife moved into the home after Mrs. Miller moved away. Young Hunt seemed to grow up overnight, bringing many more boys to play basketball in the same drive where the Miller boy washed his car. Hunt went away to college last month. Once again, I miss the sound of a basketball bouncing.

Jonathan and his brother Chris made lots of noise up the street, playing basketball and shooting firecrackers off the whole month of July. In the winter, they rode their sleds from the top of the hill past the house, laughing all the way. And all the while, Ashley played all over the neighborhood, riding bikes and playing dolls with Julia. Sometimes, they would shoot baskets with the boys and trick-or-treat in late October. They all liked to harass Charlie, the neatnik in the neighborhood. Jon died one morning after they were almost grown. He had the same heart defect that took his father. Ashley said once that Jonathan's dad, Mr. Bob, told her she could shoot baskets or come into his house anytime she wanted. It became quiet for a while after Jonathan and Mr. Bob left. Ashley and Julia were away in college. Jonathan's mom is building a new house and will move soon. There were no fireworks in our neighborhood this year; I even miss them.

There were still sounds of adult laughter coming from our backdoor neighbors on weekends. There was a group of people from the Greatest Generation, who would have cocktails before going out to dinner. There was always a lot of laughter. This group slowly melted away. That house is now empty and still. I miss that Friday night sound.

The little twin girls next door were another welcome sound. They would swing and sing songs of the 2010 vintage. They often jumped on their trampoline, laughing with friends. I understand they will soon be leaving for their new home in the country. I will miss them coming to sell cookies and of course the songs, the songs. Sweet little voices.

One day, I found a basketball under a bush; it had rolled down the hill from the baseball coach's front lawn; Phil's lawn was always filled with boys playing some sport: baseball, soccer, basketball. A little sister often watched while the family dog stood guard. They recently moved; a For Sale sign is on that lawn now. I miss seeing Phil talking to that dog.

There are long periods of stillness now; we go for long walks, listening for the sounds only children can make. We wait and wait until grandkids show up. The sounds are beautiful, but somehow, I know they won't last. Our neighbors up the hill have three grandsons who make noise for a while, but they too don't stay long.

I know now how my father felt after all the neighborhood boys left. He could still hear the sounds of kids at recess and the noon hour, echoing up the valley from the old grade school, but after a few more years, the school closed. I wish I had have written my dad a letter, but I didn't know then.

I didn't understand then why Mr. Brown wasn't angry when we broke his window with a baseball, but now I get it.

That is the way life is. Children grow up, and neighborhoods change. Cultures change, and even towns and cities change. Change is time; time is change. Time brings, and time takes away.

Wait, was that a church bell ringing? No, they don't ring much anymore, I guess it was something on TV. Maybe it was SpongeBob SquarePants.

"Then he put a little child among them. Taking the child in his arms, he said to them, 'Anyone who welcomes a little child like this on my behalf welcomes me, and anyone who welcomes me welcomes my Father who sent me'" (Mark 9:36).

1. Should we be less protective of our children and let them find adventures and explore in order to become better adults?
2. Do you ever scold neighborhood children for tramping on your flowers or grass?
3. Are we sometimes too busy watching the news or a ballgame to notice children?
4. If you had it to do over, would you spend more time watching children at play?
5. What can you do to make a small difference for children growing up?
6. Do you ever miss the sound of a church bell tolling?
7. Do you miss the sounds of children playing in the neighborhood?

Stress

Question: Think of a time when you felt great stress. How did you relieve it?

I just had a text from a friend who happens to be a Mormon. We were dealing with a slightly stressful situation, so I asked him how a good Mormon deals with stress.

He replied, "Good question. I don't know; I take a run at the end of the day." He asked me to share with him whatever I came up with.

I am pretty blank right now and stressed a bit because I only have an hour and a half to write this essay and get it to the church. I don't think running will take my problem away; besides, I am too old to run. I have prayed for God to use me to write this, and I have faith that he will send something through me, so here goes.

Today's stress was caused by my failure to start soon enough, not paying attention to my notes about appointments, and an act of God. I went to an appointment a day early because I didn't look at my notes. I didn't start early today because I went to bed late last night, and I don't know why God chose to cause a leak in the roof at my pharmacy building. Oh yes, I must remember to pick up my grandson after football practice at 5:30. I just asked Siri to set an alarm for five o'clock to remind me.

One day, I asked a pharmacy tech who was about twenty years old if she was stressed.

She replied yes, and I told her, "You don't know what stress is at age twenty. That is, unless you missed three periods and don't have a husband."

She laughed, thankfully.

Stress comes in many forms; usually, it's not the stressful situation that's important but how we react to it. Of course, preparation is important; however, Mary often gets stressed trying to be prepared. I sometimes get stressed because I didn't worry enough about being prepared. We all have to understand that we create a lot of the situations ourselves. We also should know that stress doesn't exist; only our thoughts exist. We are going to have stressful situations arise, no matter how well we plan; we can decide to let the thoughts develop that make us feel stressed, or we can choose not to let those thoughts develop. When I was stuck in a ditch one time, I thought, *Well, I have been stuck in a lot of ditches in my life, and I guess I got out of all of them because here I am in this one.*

Those stressful thoughts can result from traveling into the future, as if we already know what the future will hold. In essence, that's dealing with something that is not real. We anticipate so many uncomfortable, tragic, or embarrassing events that never happen; this takes away our energy, which could be utilized today to be happy. It's not even tragic for an unmarried woman to miss her period until pregnancy is apparent. Mary handled this situation with a good mental attitude, and Jesus resulted. We all make mistakes, but the trick is not let the mistake make us.

"Stress doesn't come from what's going on in your life; it comes from your thoughts about what's going on in your life."—Andrew J. Bernstein

What we are doing when we feel stressed is letting those thoughts about something that probably will not happen ruin the moments that are happening. When we all stress about what someone will think about us, we fail to realize that most people are not thinking about us at all. When we stress about something tragic that may befall our children or grandchildren, we are stressing about something that 99.999 percent of the time will never happen. There are always alternatives for missed deadlines. Not much in this world is worth feeling stressed about, and God has offered to carry our stressful loads, so why not take advantage of his graceful offer?

"Don't worry about anything; instead, pray about everything. Tell God what you need, and thank him for all he has done. If you do this, you will experience God's peace, which is far more wonderful than the human mind can understand. His peace will guard your hearts and minds as you live in Christ Jesus" (Philippians 4:6–7).

1. Do you think worry and anxiety is the mother of all stress?
2. God tells us not to worry about anything, so why don't all Christians obey him?
3. How do you avoid letting those thoughts that will make you feel stressed develop?
4. What is the difference between avoiding stress and just being lazy?
5. A good part of the stress we feel is about money. Have you ever been guilty of letting money be a source of stress in your life?
6. Have you ever used alcohol or pot to relieve stress? Is this okay, within limits? What if you tried prayer first?

What were those things you felt stressed about last month? Did your world end?

"I am an old man now and have known a great many troubles, but most of them never happened."—Mark Twain

Thank You for Being My Friend

Question: Is there someone you should have thanked before they left this earth?

About thirty years ago, I visited a couple with my wife and youngest daughter in their home. The man was my dad's first cousin and best friend. My brother and I called him Uncle Joe and his wife Aunt Frances. During that visit, I told them that they were always like a second mom and dad for me and my brother. I noticed this brought a broad smile to their faces. I am so happy today for that moment; however, if I could do it again, I would physically hug them. Uncle Joe and Aunt Frances are buried next to my mom and dad, but I have faith that they are all in his presence.

There are some people we cannot thank enough, just as there is a God we cannot thank enough. The sad truth is that we too often fail to thank anyone, including our God, with words and a hug. It is easy to mouth the words most of the time, but we often struggle with the hug. A hug means to embrace someone or something. We are physically, mentally, and spiritually showing love with a hug. We are humbling ourselves before someone we feel love for. Our words seem somewhat empty if we allow our ego to keep us from this act of love and thankfulness. We hug our God by hugging his children; we hug God by embracing his message and accepting his forgiveness and offer of salvation. Sometimes, we say the words without the hug. It's not just the words you speak but also tone of voice and body language that communicate authenticity—and humility is the key.

There are people (children of God) still living who we should thank for something. It may be just for being our friend. We often want to keep score in this life and resort to scoreboard we have created when evaluating friendships.

We too often say to ourselves, "They have … [or they have not …] Therefore, why should I …?" Fill in the blanks. If we develop this habit of scoring the behavior of others, we will seldom have friendships worth being truly thankful for. If God keeps score, we are all in trouble because we would not be offered the forgiveness given from the cross. Jesus did not say to the thief next to him, "You sinned, so why should I forgive you?"

The most important thing we should be thankful for is forgiveness. Without forgiveness, life could not exist in this world of sin, and we could not have eternal life without it. We cannot be truly thankful without offering forgiveness. We are constantly offering forgiveness to our spouse and children for all kinds of behavior. We do this because of the love we have for them, not because they may or may not deserve it. Our Lord does the same by his hugging grace.

This season preceding the celebration of the birth of Christ begins in our nation with our feast of Thanksgiving. Let us understand on this day that we are forgiven, and let us be truly thankful. We should not only say the words of thankfulness, we should also give the hug by forgiving others and telling them how much their friendship and love mean to us.

Thankfulness cannot exist without forgiveness.

During the Thanksgiving holiday, we focus on our blessings and express our gratitude to God for them. But thanks should be on our lips every day. We can never say thank you enough to parents, friends, and leaders and especially to God. When thanksgiving becomes an integral part of your life, you will find that your attitude toward life will change. You will become more positive, gracious, loving, and humble.

If you believe in God, then your first instinct in all things must be from gratitude: for creation, for love, for mercy.

"Gratitude is not only the greatest of virtues, but the parent of all others."—Cicero

"It is good to give thanks to the Lord, to sing praises to the Most High. It is good to proclaim your unfailing love in the morning, your faithfulness in the evening" (Psalm 92:1–2).

"But then God our Savior showed us his kindness and love. He saved us, not because of the good things we did, but because of his mercy. He washed away our sins and gave us a new life through the Holy Spirit. He generously poured out the Spirit upon us because of what Jesus Christ our Savior did. He declared us not guilty because of his great kindness. And now we know that we will inherit eternal life. These things I have told you are all true. I want you to insist on them so that everyone who trusts in God will be careful to do good deeds all the time. These things are good and beneficial for everyone" (Titus 3:4–8).

1. Why don't you tell those you love that you are thankful for what they have done for you before it is too late?
2. Do you ever fail to show love to someone because you thought they acted wrongly in the past?
3. Will you look for goodness instead of faults in those you have Thanksgiving dinner with?
4. Is it difficult for you to humble yourself and say the words "Thank you"?
5. Is it difficult for you to even tell your spouse how much they mean to you? Will you regret this if they leave this life before you?
6. What are you thankful for?

Thanks for the Memories

Question: Can you recall a special memory that you shared with a friend?

We were expecting over twenty family members for a Thanksgiving celebration, and the anticipation was causing a little stress to develop between Mary and me. I told her that we could be all getting together to bury a grandchild or another loved one. That terrible thought contrasts the arrival of family for a feast of Thanksgiving. I don't think my wisdom impressed my spouse enough for her to quit worrying about where everyone would sit and how she could make it all happen, but in my own mind, I prayed for God to not test my faith right now and thanked him for my family and friends. I don't think I have the faith and fortitude of Job and am thankful that God has not taken children or grandchildren to be with him in heaven. We do need to put things in perspective at times in order to prevent our reactions to cause harm.

Those thoughts caused me to go through all the things I am thankful for besides God's love for us. I am especially thankful for the many friends I have had and continue to make in this life. Sadly, many of those great friends have already gone to be with Jesus. I visited the gravesite of one of the most recently departed yesterday. On his new gravestone, there was a quote from his mother: "Forgiveness was in the heart of God before sin was in the heart of man." I am thankful for God's forgiveness. I am thankful for friends.

A real friend seldom needs to give or receive forgiveness because it is a given. I know that a real friend would never do or say anything to hurt me, and if they do so unintentionally, then I am quick to forgive and forget. A true friend seldom needs to be asked to help in bad situations and will be there for me. A real friend loves me in spite of my failures and thoughtlessness. A real friend finds value in me that I cannot see, and I in him as well. A real friend is someone I can trust and tell my innermost secrets, knowing they will never go elsewhere beyond my friend. A friend brings me closer to Jesus instead of leading me astray. A true friend always builds me up and never tears me down. A friend makes the effort to contact me on a regular basis, and I the same in return. A friend is someone I can sit quietly with and not feel the need to talk, because he understands me. A friend loves me in spite of me, or perhaps because I am me. It kind of sounds like I could be talking about Jesus, my best friend.

As I visited with my friend, I heard another friend call from the other end of the cemetery: "Hey, Jimmy. How about me?" I walked over to her grave, there with her husband and child. I remembered seeing that sweet little boy in his casket a few hours after he drowned one summer day. My friends kept their faith in spite of that tragedy. Then I heard another friend and another. It was starting to get dark as I went from grave to grave visiting old friends, hearing them laugh, and seeing their smiling faces. "Sorry," I said. "I will come back. I love you all. Thanks for being my friend. Thanks for the memories."

When I got home, Mary asked where I had been. I responded, "With my friends."

"I have told you this so that you will be filled with my joy. Yes, your joy will overflow! I command you to love each other in the same way that I love you. And here is how to measure it: the greatest love is shown when people lay down their lives for their friends. You are my friends if you obey me. I no longer call you servants, because a master doesn't confide in his servants. Now you are my friends, since I have told you everything the Father told me. You didn't choose me, I chose you. I appointed you to go and produce fruit that will last, so that the Father will give you whatever you ask for using my name" (John 15:11).

1. Would you give up your life for your best friend?
2. When was the last time you contacted your friend?

3. Do you tend to find faults in your friends?
4. Do you ever spread gossip about your friends?
5. When your friends are in trouble, are you there for them? What if they went to prison?
6. After someone dies, do you just forget them and not think about them anymore?

"A true friend unbosoms freely, advises justly, assists readily, adventures boldly, takes all patiently, defends courageously, and continues a friend unchangeably."—William Penn

The Back Nine

Question: Has anyone ever said or done anything that made you feel disrespected?

One day several years ago, I noticed a man sitting in the lobby of my pharmacy, just waiting patiently for his name to be called. I thought, *that gentleman has been coming here for several years and seldom speaks, just hands in his order and sits quietly.* I walked around the counter, sat across from him, and greeted him with something like, "Looks like it is going to be a long winter."

He looked up with a grin and said, "Yes, I imagine it will. I have seen worse, though."

Taking the opening to make conversation, I asked if he had been in the military during World War II. I had noticed on our computer that he was in his eighties and about the right age to have been in the service during that period.

"Yes, I was in Europe and served with General Patton during the Battle of the Bulge," he said. "1944 was one of the coldest winters in Europe. Then to add to the misery, people were trying to kill us."

The usually quiet man became a little more animated as he showed me some of the scars on his legs from wounds received during the war.

"I have never experienced any misery like we experienced that winter in Europe. There was no way to get warm and many days not even hot coffee or hot food. Didn't get a shower for two months."

Our conversation ended when I received a call, and the gentleman picked up his meds and left. I didn't see him for a few months, then one day, he came in for refills on his wife's medicine and showed me a silver dollar from 1865. I looked at the old coin and commented that it was minted the year the Civil War ended. I started to hand him the coin when he said, "No, I want you to have it. I'm just getting rid of some things."

Thinking that you should never turn down a gift, I thanked him profusely and shook hands as I accepted his offering. As he went out the door, he turned, made eye contact, and smiled. I never saw him again but read in the paper a few months later that he had died of cancer. I continue to think of those little conversations and am beginning to understand the importance of showing interest in as many people as I can as I pass through this short life. I think the silver dollar this gentleman gave me was a thank you for showing him a little attention and asking him about his war experiences.

Just this week, I answered a call from a patient at the pharmacy and was becoming a little annoyed at her slow speech and confusion. She apologized, saying she had recently suffered a stroke that had impaired her speech. Our delivery person was ill, so I offered to bring the medicine to her. After I arrived, I helped her sort through different meds from different doctors. I started to ask questions, such as did she have any family locally. She then started to tell me something about her life. She said that she and her husband went through two years of medical school to become medical missionaries. Her husband, unfortunately, was killed in Vietnam in 1968. In her recovery from this terrible loss, she changed her major and eventually graduated from NYU with a PhD in languages. This was after she graduated from Loyola University with a master's degree. She had taught Latin and religion for several years before retirement. I discovered my new friend also had Parkinson's disease as well as myasthenia gravis, a neurologic disease. She told me that she had suffered a heart attack and had a near-death experience. "They" told her that she was being sent back because she had more work to do. This was after she offered to give up because she was so tired. And I in my superior intellect was about to dismiss this accomplished Christian woman.

It seems that most of us fail to show much interest in each other, especially older people. We are so busy thinking about ourselves and our own lives, we don't have much interest in hearing about other people's lives. It is our loss not to become interested in other people's life experiences. It is when we forget ourselves that we do things that will be remembered.

I believe what most elderly people dislike about old age, beyond the physical problems, is to feel dismissed by younger people as insignificant to matters at hand. Unthinking and unkind younger people often just look past the elderly, thinking they've lost the ability to produce wise answers just because they have lost some movement and sensory capabilities. I recall an incident years ago when an old physician diagnosed appendicitis by physical examination; other young doctors had missed it by relying on lab tests that showed nothing significant. The two younger doctors looked at the older one as if he had just magically appeared. They were somewhat shocked by the value of his older techniques and experience.

I have now reached the age that most would consider elderly. I try to act younger, but my body continues to remind me that I am playing the back nine. It takes several people to have a conversation because friends my age have difficulty remembering names and places. We spend a lot of time learning where the nearest restroom is in any store we shop. As George Burns once said, "When I am tying my shoes, I stop and think if there is anything else I need to do while I am down here." Other drivers tend to honk at me a lot and sometimes give me a middle-finger salute as they pass. I tend to gather food stains on my clothing and make messes wherever I am in my home. I don't understand a lot when young people talk because of hearing impairment, and most things my wife says have to be repeated. I tend to plan the simple act of standing up and even dread it. We all experience these little insults as we age, and we should be tolerant and respectful of those older people who are experiencing impairments.

I have learned, however, that for every ability I've lost physically, I've gained many abilities, including being kind and interested in others. I've learned that it's more important to add life to my years than it is to add years to my life. I've learned that laughter, kindness, and interest in others is the best medicine. I've learned that I should do unto others as though I was one of the others. I've learned that others are not interested in me complaining about aches and pains and doctor appointments. Most people are not as interested in my grandkids and dogs as I am. There seems to be a tendency as we age to bore people by talking about ourselves and not showing interest in them. The art of conversation requires you to ask questions of the subject at hand, not using it as an opening to go on and on about personal experiences with too many uninteresting details.

As we age, we get set in our ways, not open to change or new ideas. The older people I admired from my past are the ones who were open to change and new interests. The ones I remember most are the ones with a smile on their face. The ones I try to forget are the ones who constantly talked about their problems.

Our modern American culture has allowed old people to be less respected than most other cultures in the world. Many cultures in the world honor and respect the elderly, so what happened in America? Can we as Christians do anything as individuals to change our culture?

"The wiser mind mourns less for what age takes away than what it leaves behind."—William Wordsworth, *The Fountain*

"Show your fear of God by standing up in the presence of elderly people and showing respect for the aged" (Leviticus 19:32).

1. Do you ever find yourself replacing dreams with regrets?
2. Children sometimes wet their pants, spill their food, and feel hurt by being ignored. Is it not the same for elderly people?
3. Do you ever offer too many details and change a conversation's topic without caring if the other parties are even interested in the subject you digressed to?
4. Do you ever wish you could have that conversation you failed to have with your grandparents?
5. Have you ever dismissed an older coworker because you assumed they didn't have anything cogent to offer?

The Church

Question: Why do you attend your particular church? If you don't attend any church, why not?

All of us seem to desire the cohesiveness and security of a family. Some of us have been lucky enough to have been raised in a loving, functional family. Others have been raised in more dysfunctional families and even without much love. Whether you were raised in a loving environment or not, there is still that attraction to become part of some group of like-minded humans with common desires and goals. There is a security need that is primordial. When groups are functional, there is a bonding that if nurtured develops into friendship and a form of emotional relationship that is akin to Christian love. Jesus understood this and chose his disciples with a spiritually guided wisdom that unveiled character in each with the potential necessary for his message to be carried on.

All families have dysfunction at times. This is human nature; we are imperfect, but most are seeking a more perfect life. Jesus had a message for all of us that was pretty simple, but we at times make it more complicated than necessary. He said we should love one another as we love ourselves, and we should love our God. He showed us that sacrifice is necessary, tolerance is necessary, and forgiveness is necessary. All of God's desires for human development are based upon these principles, in some sense.

In any group, there are usually some misguided individuals who can disrupt goals and the cohesiveness of that group in a thousand ways. There have to be other individuals who keep focused and are able to articulate goals well enough to keep the majority on course. I remember a phrase once used by Spiro Agnew, the vice president of the United States, which was about the only thing he ever said that made sense. He referred to those in the Fourth Estate, the press, who were disrupting President Nixon's efforts, as the "nattering nabobs of negativism." There will always be those who natter about all the negative aspects of any subject; if not confronted with enough truths, they will cause the group to lose focus.

The apostle Paul spent most of his time writing and speaking to early Christian churches about the simple concepts of Christianity and human nature. We have been taught that Satan is at the heart of evilness in human nature. Whether Satan is an entity or the absence of love, that force is in each of us, trying to pull us away from the message of Jesus.

There are thousands of Christian churches in our world, stemming from hundreds of denominations. That is probably a good thing because of the multitude of cultures, all requiring a different approach to the common goal. Some of these churches function and grow, while other wither and die. The common question is, why? The simple answer is sometimes demographics, but most of the time, it is because of loss of focus. The next question is, why do some churches lose focus?

Jesus said, "Where ever there are two or more gathered together in my name, there I will be also." I guess these can be the seeds of any church; however, for this discussion, we are talking about the developed churches. Most Christian groups that call themselves a church have some kind of leadership. They have a pastor or congregation leader of some sort. Then they have the congregation, or members of the church. I believe if the pastor is not guided by the Holy Spirit, his church will eventually fail. We are promised the necessary elements will be provided by that Spirit if called upon faithfully. Some pastors are gifted by the ability to articulate dynamically, and some are gifted more by their personal magnetism. The Holy Spirit will utilize the gifts to the fulfillment of the message, if the pastor keeps seeking and listening for spiritual guidance. Sometimes, pastors and other leaders could be led to the Spirit by the congregation.

The congregation, the laity, has an equal if not greater duty to perform for the life and growth of a church. Their duty is to seek spiritual guidance and also develop their gifts for the good of Christ's church. When we sincerely seek that spiritual guidance, we are promised that it will be given. With this Spiritual strength, we need to constantly be on guard not to allow that absence of love, that demonic part of our nature, to cause us to lose focus upon our pathway. We should not allow ourselves to be the nattering nabobs of negativism. We should constantly be seeking ways to love each other and support our pastor and thereby support the growth of our church. No family can function if negativism is the driving force instead of love. No church can survive without the Holy Spirit of God. The apostles knew this.

"And now I make one more appeal, my dear brothers and sisters. Watch out for people who cause divisions and upset people's faith by teaching things that are contrary to what you have been taught. Stay away from them" (Romans 16:17).

"A great wave of persecution began that day, sweeping over the church in Jerusalem, and all the believers except the apostles fled into Judea and Samaria. (Some godly men came and buried Stephen with loud weeping.) Saul was going everywhere to devastate the church. He went from house to house, dragging out both men and women to throw them into jail.

"But the believers who had fled Jerusalem went everywhere preaching the Good News about Jesus. Philip, for example went to the city of Samaria and told the people there about the Messiah. Crowds listened intently to what he had to say because of the miracles he did. Many evil spirits were cast out, screaming as they left their victims. And many who had been paralyzed or lame were healed. So there was great joy in that city.

"A man named Simon had been a sorcerer there for many years, claiming to be someone great. The Samaritan people, from the least to the greatest, often spoke of him as 'the Great One—the Power of God.' He was very influential because of the magic he performed. But now the people believed Philip's message of Good News concerning the Kingdom of God and the name of Jesus Christ. As a result, many men and women were baptized. Then Simon himself believed and was baptized. He began following Philip wherever he went, and he was amazed by the great miracles and signs Philip performed.

"When the apostles back in Jerusalem heard that the people of Samaria had accepted God's message, they sent Peter and John there. As soon as they arrived, they prayed for these new Christians to receive the Holy Spirit. The Holy Spirit had not yet come upon any of them, for they had only been baptized in the name of the Lord Jesus. Then Peter and John laid their hands upon these believers, and they received the Holy Spirit.

"When Simon saw that the Holy Spirit was given when the apostles placed their hands upon people's heads, he offered money to buy this power. 'Let me have this power too,' he exclaimed, 'so that when I lay my hands on people they will receive the Holy Spirit!'

"But Peter replied, 'May your money perish with you for thinking God's gift can be bought'" (Acts 8:1–21).

1. Can any Christian continue to grow without the Holy Spirit being called upon?
2. How do we receive the Holy Spirit? Does it have to be in a symbolic form by the laying on of hands?
3. Why do we fear receiving the Holy Spirit? Is it because people sometimes act misguided or overzealous? Is it because we fear our responsibility will increase?
4. Do you think that some Christians do not want to be disturbed and challenged in their faith? How about you?
5. Do you think that some churches are more Spirit-filled than others? Are some just not guided by the Holy Spirit?
6. Are you one to just sit back and complain about how things are in your church and never try to ask the Holy Spirit to give you guidance concerning your responsibility?
7. If the pastor fails to inspire you, what do you think you should do about it? Get him moved, or examine your own spirit?
8. Have you ever walked into a church, sat down, crossed your arms, and said in your mind, *Okay, preacher, inspire me.*

The Holy Spirit already dwells in each of us; all we have to do is recognize this source of power, and we can do great things for the Lord. A simple prayer opens that pathway to strength, love, understanding, and courage.

Lord, I give my life to you. Amen.

The Devil Made Me Do It

Question: Do You Believe There Is a Satan?

During the sixties, comedian Flip Wilson had a character in one of his routines who repeated the phrase "The devil made me do it." We may have even used this as an excuse sometime in our youth. If we didn't verbalize it, we may have thought it so.

Newton's third law of motion states that when a body exerts a force on a second body, the second body simultaneously exerts a force equal in magnitude and opposite in direction of the first body. We humans tend to understand that there is usually something the opposite of most things we are exposed to daily. There is light and dark, there is hot and cold, up and down, and so on. It therefore follows that if there is a God, there must be a devil. We all agree for the most part that there exists good and evil in the world. Good is related to God, and therefore evil must be attributed to an entity called the devil, or Satan. Since dark is really the absence of light, could it follow that evil is only the absence of good? Cold is the absence of heat; perhaps the devil only exists to define the polar opposite of goodness, or God. Does it really matter if Satan exists as an entity, or is it just a name we give to evilness?

Our Bible refers to Satan and the devil at least seventeen times as the adversary of God, the personification of evil, and the enemy of everything good. It helps most of us to have a face of some kind for most concepts in order to deal with them, but I wonder if we need to think of Satan as a being in the sense of a powerful spirit that has demonic intentions for you and me. We use the devil to teach children about evil in the world; I wonder if we should create fear in their little minds that there is some kind of monster that exists and wants to do us harm. Would it not be better to teach children that evil acts are choices that some people make and cause harm to others?

Many Christians say it doesn't matter what one decides to think about Satan; the Bible says he exists, so he exists as a powerful spiritual entity capable of becoming physical. An answer would be that as long as we have the Holy Spirit, it doesn't matter whether the devil exists as an entity or just the absence of good or God. Evil exists because of the absence of good. If we strive to fill our life with good, there is no room for evil. The old adage "Idle minds are the devil's workshop" is true nonetheless.

There are references in the Bible to people becoming filled by evil spirits; Jesus even exorcised some from an individual and drove them into a herd of swine. Even in modern times, there are believable stories about possessions and exorcisms. I know a young man who was leading a free spirit lifestyle using drugs, alcohol, and sex for his pleasure when suddenly, one night, he was confronted by what he described as Satan. The experience frightened him so much that he immediately went home, awakened his parents, and even crawled in bed between them, in tears. He was changed by the experience, and he dedicated his life to helping young people find God.

The great lie of Satan is to tell us that he doesn't exist. I would guess that we would be best served to not believe this lie and accept that Satan exists and often uses seemingly beautiful things to entice us away from our loving God.

When I did evil things in my life, I would say, "The devil made me do it." However, I believe I always had the choice to do good or evil deeds. I am ultimately responsible for my own acts.

Jesus warned Simon Peter that Satan would like to destroy his faith, but he had prayed for him, and his faith would prevail.

"Simon, Simon, Satan has asked to have all of you, to sift you like wheat. But I have pleaded in prayer for you, Simon that your faith should not fail. So when you have repented and turned to me again, strengthen and build up your brothers" (Luke 22:31–32).

1. Have you ever felt the presence of evil or the devil?
2. If you deny the existence of Satan, do you also deny God, in some sense?
3. Do you think some people fear evil or Satan so much they don't live a happy life?
4. Why do we sometimes talk about a child with a sparkle in our eye and say, "That little rascal is full of the devil"?
5. Does God ever let us be tempted by Satan so that our faith will grow?
6. When we witness people doing such cruel and horrible things to others, there can be no other answer than Satan exists, or do you believe that a human created by God is capable of horrible evil without Satan?

"The world is a dangerous place not because of people who do evil but because of people that don't do anything about it."—Albert Einstein

The Final Answer (Or, What Was Your Question?)

Question: What bit of wisdom would you give your children or grandchildren?

We were sitting around the pool at the cabin, and I was waxing eloquently when I noticed all the kids, grandkids, and cousins were listening to me. They all in their own way were fascinated by my words that day, so I took advantage of the moment.

I told them that I had always been fascinated by time: what it is and how we use it. I mean the time spent here in this universe. I've used this basic question about time to become as informed as I could along life's path. Early on, I realized that life is short (shorter for some than for others). I still don't know why that is God's way, but it is. The luck of the draw. What is important is how we utilize the time allotted to us.

I learned from my dad education is important: not just book learning but learning by observation. You can learn a lot by watching and listening to successful people. The trick is to understand what success really is. In this life, we often think money is the most valuable marker of success. Wisdom or money can get you almost anything, but it's important to know that only wisdom can save your life. A wise person is stronger than the ten richest people in town.

It is not that money is a bad thing; it can be a good thing if we use it properly and share a little when we can. I've learned a few things as I fumbled along and mucked my way through this life. I learned that even the most evil man in town can have a fine funeral, with lots of people saying good things about him, but a poor man may have only a few attend his service, even if he was good. Some people live a good life and seem to be punished with sorrow and pain, while others can live an evil life and enjoy all the earthly pleasures before departing. This life does not always seem to be just.

I have observed something else in this world of ours: The fastest runner doesn't always win the race, and the strongest football team doesn't always win the game. The wise are often poor, and the skillful are not necessarily wealthy. And those who are educated don't always lead successful lives. It is all decided by chance, by being at the right place at the right time.

I have noticed that the quiet words of a wise person are better than the shouts of a foolish king. A wise person can overcome weapons of war, but a sinner can destroy much that is good. My dad always said to be careful in business; it does no good to charm a snake after it has bitten you. However, if your boss is mad at you, don't quit; a quiet spirit can overcome even great mistakes. He always said that you will sleep better knowing you kept your temper quiet.

Dad also said, "Don't eavesdrop on others; you may hear someone laughing at you. For you know how often you've laughed at others."

We all make mistakes. Only one man who ever lived was perfect. Dad said, "Take all of life in. Enjoy every minute of it. But remember that you must give God an accounting for everything you do."

Back at the cabin, I told my audience that I'd tried my best to let wisdom guide my thoughts and actions. I was determined to be wise. But it didn't always work; wisdom is always distant and very difficult to find. I searched everywhere, determined to find wisdom and understand the reason for things. I was determined to prove to myself that wickedness is stupid and that foolishness is madness.

I've learned that life is short and I should enjoy the fruits of my labors. We are all going to die; therefore, enjoy life while you can. Those who do not believe in an afterlife might as well wear nice clothes, drink a little wine with a happy heart, even wear a dash of cologne. Because that is all they will get. Enjoy youth before old age takes that enjoyment away. Just do it all in moderation and avoid chasing the wind. If you keep waiting for perfect conditions, you will never get anything done.

The most important thing I've learned is, don't let the excitement of youth cause you to forget your creator. Honor him in your youth before you grow old and no longer enjoy living.

"Fear God and obey his commands, for this is the duty of every person. God will judge us for everything we do, including every secret thing, whether good or bad" (Ecclesiastes 1:12; read the complete book).

It seems that Solomon had these thoughts before me.

1. Have you ever read the complete book of Ecclesiastes?
2. Do you think it is okay to enjoy life and party a little?
3. Can you think of someone who seemed to enjoy all the pleasures of this life and died without knowing God?
4. Some of us never want to give up the pleasures of youth and let them drag us down into sin. Are you like that?
5. Have you ever known someone who was very wise but not wealthy?
6. Would not the best example of someone who was very wise but not wealthy be Jesus?

The Land of the Discarded

Question: Do you tend to throw things away, or are you someone who saves many things because you may need it later?

I've been to Europe five times, and I have observed something different about all the countries I've visited. In Europe, there seems to be more preservation of homes and buildings. In Sicily, several generations lived in the same home. Sometimes, another level has been built to accommodate the growing family, but I visited several people who lived in the home of their grandparents or great-grandparents. In some homes, the interior was modern with modern furniture, but in others, even the furniture seemed ancient. I noticed that the buildings were built of stone and were built to last centuries. The streets were made of stone also and looked worn but clean. When I was in Paris, we had dinner one night in a restaurant that had been in business for over two hundred years in the same location. We also enjoyed a fine Bordeaux wine that was thirty years old. In the city of Dubrovnik, Croatia, I visited a pharmacy that had been in the same location since the fifteenth century.

In our country, we don't have as much reverence for old buildings; we tend to use materials that are not intended to last for centuries. We often have a disregard for most old things, even old people. We discard old towns and sometimes appear to discard our old people. In the name of progress, we seem to find it necessary to move mom or dad into a nursing home instead of taking care of them in our homes or providing for their care in their own homes. I realize that that is sometimes the only option. Maybe they only have one child available to provide for their care, and the child has to work. However, I believe we sometimes put people in nursing homes because we just don't want to be bothered. I don't condemn people for making this choice, but it seems that our society has developed a disregard for most things old. Automobiles are built to last only a few years because of our American desire for newness. Most of the electronic equipment we use today is made to be disposed of instead of being repaired if they don't function properly. Clothing is discarded because we want something new, not because it is worn out. The southern part of Illinois where I was born and raised has been discarded. My hometown no longer exists, unlike San Cipirello, Sicily, which was approximately the same size but has existed since Roman times.

I've noticed in my later years that there is not much respect for the elderly in our workforce. Many of us have been able to retire early, but many others work at their profession longer than younger minds will allow. There has developed a disregard of the wisdom that only comes from age and experience. With computers, we have instant access to information, which we often mistake for wisdom. Computers may give business owners demographic information that says they should move their company elsewhere, but they don't mention the human element that will suffer with that change. A century ago, a physician would usually practice in a town for his whole professional life. Most of the people in that town would have been brought into the world with the aid of that physician. Today, he may have to go wherever the corporation he works for sends him. Advice from older people is not often sought in America because the young see no value in their counsel. Most banks were once locally owned but have been bought up by large corporations, which don't have much regard for the communities they serve. The boards of these local banks which once were successful businessmen have been replaced by younger people. The newer boards don't know the community as well. Many banks have eliminated local boards. Teachers today are much younger than a century ago. In earlier times, the teacher who taught you may very well have taught your parents. History is a subject that our schools have little regard for today. We seem to have lost something as a society by not retaining older teachers who had wisdom. The teachers of old often saw their profession in a different light and had much respect for their responsibility to help create inquisitive minds.

In our process of discarding anything old, we have also discarded many values that have made our world better. This is one thing that seemed to begin in Europe and has filtered into the United States. In Europe, Christianity declined in perceived value over the years. Many churches are almost empty or only filled by older people. This trend has unfortunately developed here since World War II. There was a time in America when going to church for Sunday worship was not an option. It was required not only by church doctrine but also by parents who saw the value in religious training and worship.

I am reminded of the quote "Christianity if untrue is of little importance, but if true, it is of infinite importance" (C. S. Lewis). All Christian principles point to the value of wisdom and honoring our elderly. New ideas have value, as things change in our world, but moral values promoted by Jesus are eternal. In every aspect of our lives, we should continually be asking, does this decision fit with the values of Christ?

God gives wisdom and victory to the godly but not to those drifting through life or acting irresponsibly with his gifts and resources.

"My child. Listen to me and treasure my instructions. Tune your ears to wisdom, and concentrate on understanding. Cry out for insight and understanding. Search for them as you would for lost money or hidden treasure. Then you will understand what it means to fear the Lord, and you will gain knowledge of God. For the Lord grants wisdom! From his mouth come knowledge and understanding. He grants a treasure of good sense to the godly. He is their shield, protecting those who walk with integrity. He guards the paths of justice and protects those who are faithful to him.

"Then you will understand what is right, just, and fair and you will know how to find the right course of action every time. For wisdom will enter your heart and knowledge will fill you with joy. Wise planning will watch over you. Understanding will keep you safe" (Proverbs 2:1–11).

1. Do your grandchildren ever seek your advice? Do you ever feel disregarded by youth?
2. When you were young, did you ever seek advice from an elder?

3. Do you feel safer when the president is younger or older?
4. Do you feel safer with an older pilot on an airline or a young one? Why?
5. Have you ever had a younger boss? Did you learn from him?
6. Was your favorite teacher younger than thirty?
7. Is wisdom limited to the elderly?
8. Would you be on the side of preservation or removal of an older building in favor of a modern one?

The Last Great Generation?

Question: What do you think set your generation apart from the others?

My generation doesn't really have a name, like the most recent generation, the millennials, the name the news media has given those born between 1981 and 2000. We didn't have our own music; we had to claim some of the greatest generation's music, the big bands. Then there was a little of doo-wop and rock and roll. I think we may have just been a generation without our own music. I recently read an article written for marketing people that called those born between 1927 and 1945 the Matures or the Silents. We didn't protest or cause disruption. We were disciplined, self-sacrificing, and cautious. We are one generation of the six generations living today. This article stated that each generation as a generalization has different likes, dislikes, and attributes and as a common group has similarities.

Each generation has a responsibility to guide the succeeding ones from the lessons it learned. With this in mind, it appears to me that my generation has failed in some ways to educate and create an understanding of self-discipline, government, and God. We failed to teach respect, faith, and loyalty. My generation respected our parents, teachers, and police. We were loyal to our employers, even corporations. The succeeding generations show less respect for all authority; they want to live their lives without anyone telling them what is right and what is wrong. They dress slovenly if they choose and speak with similar language. They don't respect traditions and institutions of the past because they think they're too restrictive. The millennials believe previous generations were reckless with the environment and the earth's resources. They believe they are the fixers, while we believe they've been given much without much effort on their own, be it money, automobiles, clothing, electronic devices, or freedom to make decisions. They demand proof of things that were generally accepted by previous generations, choosing not to accept them on faith.

My generation got in trouble for chewing gum in class, and the latest generations get in trouble for massacring their fellow students. There is an anger among youth today we cannot understand. Perhaps they see us as stupid because we are not as computer savvy or slow to accept new electronics; therefore, we're also unable to understand that the world has changed and is changing too rapidly for us. If we are so uninformed and unadapting, we should not be allowed to restrict their behavior. If we do try to restrict their behavior, they become angry and often react in inappropriate or violent ways.

I fear that many in the latest generations may be unable to understand the difference between what is real and what appears to be real in their electronic world. We have developed electronics that can produce virtual reality. I wonder if the so-called gamers who have made electronic game-playing the center of their lives sometimes believe the roles they play in the games are real. Young people playing war games and taking on the role of a commander and destroying enemies may resent their mothers telling them to brush their teeth or do their homework.

My generation sees value in attending church, while the succeeding generations are increasingly not attending church. Many resent the discipline required by Christianity and dismiss the wisdom and values created by centuries of cultural development and teaching by the church. The millennials are used to a rapidly moving world with rapid rewards. Perhaps they believe wisdom can be acquired rapidly also. They depend on a computer to process information that used to be processed by humans. This process is where wisdom develops in humans.

"These are evil times, and this evil generation keeps asking me to show them a miraculous sign. But the only sign I will give them is the sign of the prophet Jonah. What happened to him was a sign to the people of Nineveh that God has sent me, the Son of Man, to these people.

"The queen of Sheba will rise up against this generation on judgment day and condemn it, because she came from a distant land to hear the Wisdom of Solomon. And now someone greater than Solomon is here, and you refuse to listen to him. The people of Nineveh, too, will rise up against this generation on judgment day and condemn it, because they repented at the preaching of Jonah. And now someone greater than Jonan is here, and you refuse to repent" (Luke 11:29–32).

1. God asked Jonah to preach repentance to the Gentiles to show salvation was not only for the Jews but everyone. Do we fail today to even try to teach about the salvation Christ died for?
2. The queen of Sheba traveled a long distance to hear the wisdom of Solomon, who was full of faults, and yet she turned to God. Do you think you are too full of faults to try to offer Christ to nonbelievers?
3. Were the Jews punished for not accepting Christ by the Holocaust?
4. We are told by many today not to try to change another man's religion, even those in Isis. If the evil men of Nineveh, the capital of Assyria, were preached to by Jonah and repented, why should we not preach to them today?
5. Are we continuing to fail to teach our youth about Jesus?
6. Have we allowed Christian values to dissipate in our culture because of political correctness?

The Most Important Decision You Can Make

Question: What do you think was the most important decision you ever made?

I recently read that the most important decision you make in life is who to marry. This statement obviously has merit, but with closer thought, you may find such a sweeping answer will not stand as a universal truth. Actually, the most important decision anyone can make in this life is the decision to follow Christ Jesus.

The disciples of Jesus all had doubts about his message and even his divinity, up to and even after his Crucifixion. Most of them abandoned Jesus during his arrest and denied association with him. After his resurrection, they were all amazed, even though he had told them what would happen. Thomas had made no pretense about his disbelief. It would be after Jesus appeared to him and had him place his fingers into his wounds that Thomas became a true believer. Those of us today may have doubts about Jesus, sometimes because of our ignorance or our failure to study and pray. We are sometimes faced with what seem to be insurmountable arguments against faith in our Lord Jesus. What we should do at these times is utilize these assaults upon our faith to build a stronger faith. Jesus did not berate Thomas for his disbelief but used that disbelief to demonstrate to the other disciples that he was what he had said he was.

The disciples were provided empirical evidence so that they would have no doubts when the Holy Spirit descended upon them, so they could spread his word. Today, two thousand years after these events, we can have faith because of our trust in these disciples. If any of us today have little faith in

Jesus or his disciples who spread his word, we should consider this: Jesus was either a lunatic who was completely deranged, or he was who he said he was. He provided empirical evidence to the disciples so they would go out to the world strengthened by the Holy Spirit. If they ever had doubts about the divinity of Jesus, they never let those doubts change their strong faith. Eleven of the twelve were martyred in horrible and painful ways, going to their death carrying faith in the promises of Jesus. If Jesus was a lunatic, then he also chose followers who would be liars and lunatics as well. For what purpose did all of them die, except for truth and the love of Jesus?

Jesus allows disbelief if we utilize that disbelief to strengthen our faith by more study, thought, and prayer. We should think of ourselves as disciples today strengthened by the Holy Spirit and the words and lives of the apostles.

When I was twelve, I became the first in my family to accept Jesus. I had the courage provided by the Holy Spirit to lead my family to church. At a later time in my life, I was leading many in the wrong direction but always feeling that spiritual anchor of Jesus holding on to me. I have learned much from my mistakes and understand that we leave something behind with whoever we come face-to-face with. Our Christ mission is to make sure that what we leave with everyone is love. We may be twelve or twelve hundred; we may be constrained to a hospital bed or even a prison, but if we are conscious, we can spread the love of Jesus.

"So be truly glad! There is wonderful joy ahead, even though it is necessary for you to endure many trials for a while.

"These trials are only to test your faith, to show that it is strong and pure. It is being tested as fire tests and purifies gold, and your faith is far more precious to God than mere gold. So if your faith remains strong after being tried by fiery trials, it will bring you much praise and glory and honor on the day when Jesus Christ is revealed to the whole world.

"You love him even though you have never seen him. Though you do not see him, you trust him, and even now you are happy with a glorious, inexpressible joy. Your reward for trusting him will be the salvation of your souls" (1 Peter 1:8-9).

1. Doesn't the fact that you're reading this tell you that you seek faith? Why should you leave your quest here?
2. If Jesus was a lunatic and his followers were equally deranged, how is it possible that such a great hoax based upon lunacy to survive scrutiny for two thousand years?
3. If you are a betting man and bet that Jesus was a lunatic, you are wagering everything; if you win, you'll win nothing, but you'll lose everything. However, if you bet that Jesus is what he says he is and win, you'll win everything.
4. Jesus has his hand extended, no matter where you are, so why not accept his offer of salvation?
5. No matter where you are, if you're in darkness, Jesus provides a lamp; why not turn it on?

"I can do all things through Christ who strengthens me" (Philippians 4:13).

The Deaths of the Apostles

All except one of the twelve apostles died as martyrs during the first century AD. Only John died a natural death.

The possible causes of death of each of the twelve apostles:

Andrew: Martyrdom by crucifixion (bound, not nailed, to a cross).

Bartholomew: Martyrdom by being either beheaded or flayed alive and crucified, head downward.

James the Greater: Martyrdom by being beheaded or stabbed with a sword.

James the Lesser: Martyrdom by being thrown from a pinnacle of the Temple at Jerusalem, then stoned and beaten with clubs.

John: Died of old age.

Jude: Martyrdom by being beaten to death with a club.

Judas: Suicide.

Matthew: Martyrdom by being burned, stoned, or beheaded.

Peter: Martyrdom by crucifixion with his head downwards.

Philip: Martyrdom.

Simon: Martyrdom by crucifixion or being sawn in half.

Thomas: Martyrdom by being stabbed with a spear.

The Power of the Spirit

Question: Can you think of an experience that gave you a profound understanding and empathy you did not have before?

About fifty years ago, I fell into a depression after we lost a baby late in the pregnancy. A new drug had just come on the market for treating depression, and I recovered after a few weeks of therapy. During my depressive state, I experienced all the classic symptoms of clinical depression, which I still remember to this day. I have never been clinically depressed since that experience, but I developed an empathy and understanding of what others are experiencing when they are truly depressed. This experience enhanced my skills as a pharmacist when counseling patients taking antidepressants.

In the mid-sixties, I attended a four-day retreat in Kansas City designed to create a spiritual awakening for those seeking a boost to their Christian faith. Some attendees left the retreat because they didn't really want to give their lives completely to Christ. I was searching for something missing in my life and offered my spirit to God to experience whatever was going to happen in those four days. During the process of fasting, silence, prayer, preaching, companionship, meditation, discussion, singing, and testimonials, I became filled with the Holy Spirit in a way that made me feel fortified. When I came home, I was ready to live a life for Christ in a way I had never understood before. Music in church became more vivid, sermons held more meaning than ever, and the scriptures filled my soul. I understood worship and prayer with an enlightened enhancement. I began to love my family and friends in a more complete way. My light began to shine more brightly than ever before. The phrase "Spirit filled" had a meaning I never understood before.

I soon discovered that while I had changed, the world did not change. My enthusiasm was opposed by many friends, and I soon learned to temper my efforts to save the world in order to become a more effective advocate for Jesus. During the next few years, I studied, prayed, and loved as I never had before. As I climbed my spiritual ladder, I discovered the wall the ladder was leaning against had demons lurking behind it. The higher I climbed, the thinner the wall seemed. In spite of the blessings God had been giving me and in spite of the life I was living for Christ, I fell for the devil's offerings. I soon turned my back to Christ and lived a selfish, worldly life. This led to a divorce and pain to the very people I had loved so much.

God held on to me, even though I was trying to hide from him. For several years, I did not go to church, but I did pray for help. After several years in the wilderness of sin, I was blessed with a new wife and another wonderful daughter. It took a few years of quiet example from my wife and daughter before I was led back to church and slowly recovered my Christian life. I never lost the ability to feel a fellowship with spirit-filled Christians; I just avoided them because I was lost in the pleasures of the world. Jesus never gave up on me, and I was slowly brought back to the faith. I know this was because of my prayers and the prayers of family and friends.

I understand what spirit filled means more than ever, and I also understand that to maintain this fullness of the spirit, I need to be vigilant and pray about everything. A new Christian is somewhat like a new physician. After physicians complete their formal training, they must continually feed their knowledge and hone their skills; likewise, Christians have to continually feed their spirit.

God continually answers my prayers, sometimes in miraculous ways. In the humility of a spirit-filled life, which is not perfect but growing, I try to utilize what gifts I have. I believe God wants me to bring others to understand the joy of releasing completely to trusting the Holy Spirit.

We must understand that to be spirit-filled does not mean we will never make mistakes or sin again. We will, however, be more fortified against fear, worry, and embarrassment of our faith. The spirit will lead us in ways we cannot imagine when we release control of our lives to God.

There is a mutual feeling of understanding and love between those filled with the spirit; this is what God wants all of us to experience.

The question many will have is, how do I become spirit-filled? The simple answer is to accept Jesus Christ as your personal savior and offer yourself to him without reservations. You will not become a perfect Christian immediately, but you will hunger for your vessel to be filled. We fill them through study, prayer, introspection, meditation, and actions. The results will be a more profound awareness, among other things. You will hear God speaking to you through your pastor's sermons. Scriptures will have more meaning. God's music will become more beautiful. Most of all, love will become easier and more desirable. You will find more joy in life and see the petals on a rose instead of the thorns. You will see goodness in people more than faults.

People who don't listen to their physician should save their time and their doctor's time. The same is true when seeking spiritual healing from the Great Physician. Trust is the key. Offer your life to God, and then trust him completely.

"When you follow the desires of your sinful nature, your lives will produce these evil results: sexual immorality, impure thoughts, and eagerness for lustful pleasure. Idolatry, participation in demonic activities, hostility, quarreling, jealousy, outbursts of anger, selfish ambition, divisions, the feeling that everyone is wrong except those in your own little group, envy, drunkenness, wild parties, and other kinds of sin. Let me tell you again as I have before, that anyone living that sort of life will not inherit the Kingdom of God.

"But when the Holy Spirit controls our lives, he will produce this kind of fruit in us: love, joy, peace, patience, kindness, goodness, faithfulness, gentleness, and self-control. Here there is no conflict with the law" (Galatians 5:19–22).

1. What part of your life are you afraid to offer to God?
2. Do you fear God asking you to do something you don't want to do?
3. Do you deny certain things you do that may be of a sinful nature?
4. Do you want to be a very active Christian or not?
5. Do you look for faults in other people instead of good qualities?
6. Do you have a problem trusting anyone, including God?
7. Is it easier for you to trust and love animals instead of humans?

My Prayer

I lay all my responsibilities at your feet. I am now yielding my heart, mind, and strength to your awesome power and glory. I desperately need you.

Open my eyes, ears, heart, and soul so that I'm not too busy to hear you. Teach me to walk, live, and be in the center of your will for my life. Use me as a blessing in the lives of my children, dear Lord.

Forgive me for my past mistakes and sins. I've been impatient, short tempered, and self-righteous, and it has made me a difficult person to love and live with. Lord, starting today, fill me with the fruit of the Holy Spirit: patience, kindness, humility, and gentleness.

Make me a person who is not easily angered; guard me from being rude or selfish. Fill me with the strength to endure all things necessary. Your perfect love never fails. I praise you, and I thank you for saving me. Amen

"I thirsted, hungered, yearned.
You touched me, and I burned.
How late I came to you.
Beauty ever ancient, ever new.
How late I came to you."—St. Augustine

The Ripple of Evil

Question: Do you think you have any racial prejudices?

I was four years old on that Christmas morning when the old telephone at my grandparents' home rang. Their ring was a short, a long, and a short. Party lines required you to listen for your particular ring. In those days, if the telephone rang on Christmas Day, it was usually not good news, because everyone we cared about was with us.

My grandmother answered the phone; she asked a few questions and then turned to the waiting adults and whispered, "Inez Bride was raped this morning."

I didn't know what *raped* meant, but it must have been something serious because of the look of shock on everyone's face. Soon, the adults were gathered together, listening to Grandmother explain that it was the Brides' hired hand, Jacob, who had committed the evil deed. It seemed that he had waited for Mr. Bride to go down to the dairy barn and then slipped into the house, grabbing Mrs. Bride. Inez was a beautiful young lady, only about five feet tall, and Jacob was pretty scary. He was a large man with bulging eyes. Dad said his hands were so rough, you could strike a kitchen match on them.

This terrible message had been delivered by our telephone operator, Ms. Combs. Ms. Combs was the conveyer of news for most of the community, anytime something important happened. We learned later that Mrs. Bride had tricked Jacob into thinking she was going to get her purse and then jumped through the window, escaping. Jacob had told her he was going to take her with him after he raped her, and she had told him they would need money; when she went for her purse, she fled out the window.

There were more phone messages that afternoon to which we younger children only gave perfunctory attention. Later, our dad and some other men got together with the sheriff to track down Jacob. Dad went home to put on warm clothes and retrieve his shotgun pistol. He then joined the group of men at the Bride farm to begin the search.

Our Christmas celebration was subdued that afternoon as the women talked quietly in the kitchen. My brother and cousins played games in the living room by the tree. It was snowing lightly outside and would have been a perfect Christmas, if not for that mysterious event of evil that affected everything.

That evening, we returned home with our mother and waited for dad. Mom seemed to be particularly anxious as we waited. My brother and I went to bed at about the usual bedtime, while Mom waited most of the night for Dad's return. It was the next afternoon when our dad finally returned. I ran out to greet him, asking many questions about the manhunt: "Did you catch Jacob? Were you scared? Where did you catch him? Did you shoot him?"

Dad only told me that they had tracked him all night and finally found him in a haystack that morning. He said ol' Jake smelled so bad, they probably could have tracked him without the dogs. After Dad walked into the house, I slipped into his 1941 Ford truck and began to study the shotgun pistol he had left on the seat. I broke it down, as I had seen him do before, and found some shells in the glove box. I put one into the chamber and closed it with a click. Just then, Dad came out and grabbed the gun, chasing me into the house.

Mom had a warm meal prepared for us, and we sat down to listen to Dad's adventure. He said that ol' Jake ran across several fields on Christmas Day, traveling perhaps seven or eight miles, heading for the Ohio River. Dad described the fear in Jacob's face as he saw Mr. Bride coming with a rope to hang him. Before he could get him hung, the sheriff caught up with them and took Jake into his custody. My brother and I were spellbound with this exciting story we had only seen the likes of at the Roxy Theater in Mounds, Illinois. Our own dad, a part of a posse, just like the cowboys in the movies.

After supper, we watched as Dad cleaned up from his night of running after dogs on the trail. His face showed the stress of the frightening night and chase. Mom soon got my brother and me ready for bed, and we all retired to the bedroom in our little one-bedroom house. George and I were in the middle of Mom and Dad's bed when George discovered the shotgun pistol Dad had carelessly tossed upon the bed. Fascinated by the long barrel, George cocked the gun and pointed it at our mother as she entered the room. Time stood still as I anticipated the loud noise about to happen.

Dad suddenly came to his senses and grabbed the gun from George's hands. "Don't ever point a gun at anyone," he scolded, "even if it isn't loaded." He quickly un-cocked the gun and broke it down. The shell I had innocently inserted earlier was ejected. All eyes turned to me as Mom and Dad wilted upon the side of the bed. The resulting lecture was unnecessary because something already told me my action had been wrong.

I've remembered that terrible series of events now for over seventy years, along with lessons about how evil will cause effects that no one can anticipate. I've thought about what could have happened if there had been a lynching. Would our dad have gone to prison for involvement? I've thought about how our lives would have changed if Dad had not grabbed the gun in time, how my brother would have been traumatized, along with Dad and myself. There was Mrs. Inez Bride, who had to live with that day her whole life. No one in our community could ever look at her without thinking about what happened. I've thought about Jacob Johnson, who spent the rest of his life in the state prison. I wondered if he went to heaven, or was he punished for eternity for his act. How was Mr. and Mrs. Bride's relationship changed because of his evil act? They never had children; was it because of Jacob's evil act on a Christmas morning?

Evil is not isolated; it ripples through space and time. Evil seeks every vacuum that is left by the absence of love.

"There is no longer Jew or Gentile, slave or free, male or female. For you are all Christians—you are one in Christ Jesus" (Galatians 3:28).

"Stop judging others, and you will not be judged. For others will treat you as you treat them. Whatever measure you use in judging others, it will be used to measure how you are judged" (Matthew 7:1–2).

1. If a man such as Jacob raped your wife, would you be tempted to kill him if you had the chance? What if he raped your daughter or granddaughter?
2. Would you punish a child or grandchild for loading a gun? How?
3. Jacob came up for parole after serving twenty years, but Mr. and Mrs. Bride successfully fought his parole request. Would you have done the same?
4. Should Jacob Johnson have received the death penalty? Would you change your opinion if you heard that Jacob started a prison ministry and saved many souls for Jesus?
5. In your mind, was Jacob Johnson white or black? Does that change any of your answers? Do you think you have any prejudices?
6. Were those who wanted to hang Jacob guilty of sin? If Mr. Bride had walked in on the act and killed Jacob, would that have been different from lynching him? What if my father had shot him running away that night? What if he was convicted and executed? If he was black, would you answer differently than if he was white?

The Root of All Evil

Question: What do you believe was the root cause of most of the evil you observed?

When I was in the first grade, my teacher was a large lady with white hair she kept braided and wrapped in a bun. Ms. Beulah also had second, third, and fourth grades in the same room. It was 1943, and the world was at war. My dad was waiting to go, following most of his friends and male relatives under thirty-five, who had already been drafted. The world was in turmoil because of tyrants seeking power over their own nation and other nations. I respected the powers that controlled my young life and accepted that most knew what was better for me than I did at that young age. Our school was segregated, as were most schools in the South (and some in the North).

One day, Ms. Beulah was on some kind of tirade about African Americans, when a very brave and wise girl named Charmaine Bryant spoke up for them.

Charmaine said, "Ms. Beulah, I think that they are just as good as we are."

Ms. Beulah's face turned red as she shouted, "There may be an African American as good as Charmaine Bryant, but there will never be an African American as good as Ms. Beulah."

I am ashamed to say that I probably laughed or cheered along with the rest of the room. Charmaine was suspended from school for two weeks.

Since that day long ago, I have become wiser and better educated and hopefully a better Christian. I have grown to understand that power can be misused in so many ways that are wrong-headed and even evil. I have learned that it is very difficult to stand up against power and even more difficult to stand up against power that has popular backing. Just as my friend Charmaine paid for her strength and wisdom in a small way, many people who had the strength to stand up against the evil going on in Nazi-controlled Germany were killed, along with the Jews, Gypsies, and gays. We in America would take another few years before we really understood the evil that was wrought by the Nazis. It would be even longer before we understood the evil we were allowing in the United States.

I have come to understand the real root of most evil is the love and misuse of power. Many bosses misuse their power over their employees. Politicians often misuse their power, which is granted by the people. Ministers of the gospels sometimes misuse the power granted them. And even schoolteachers, policemen, husbands, wives, mothers, fathers, and others sometimes misuse power.

I guess some caveman millions of years ago discovered that he had the power to get more of the meat and the best of the women by using power. Someone stronger might have taken his power away when it was being misused. Alliances need to be formed to have enough power to defeat a tyrant, and this continues to this day.

People often seek power so that they can gain wealth and then sometimes use that wealth wrongly. There are occasions when a person of strength and wisdom seeks power to right wrongs being perpetrated. Ronald Reagan had a simple attitude to correct the wrongs of the Evil Empire of the Soviet Union; he said simply, "We win; they lose." He then used his power of persuasion to convince the Soviets and others to see the world through his eyes.

Jesus was granted unbelievable power from his Father to convince the world to see the love of God through his eyes. He stood up against the power of the Jewish leaders and the Roman Empire with very little support. He had no armies, no weapons, and no great wealth; only the love and support of his Father and his message spread around the world. We could have that same power if we would only open our minds and hearts to the Holy Spirit and continue to transform the world with his power.

I continue to gain strength from a little girl who stood up to power many years ago. God forgive me for not standing up with her that day.

"If you love me, obey my commandments. And I will ask the Father, and he will give you another Counselor, who will never leave you. He is the Holy Spirit, who leads into all truth. The world at large cannot receive him, because he lives with you now and later will be in you. No, I will not abandon you as orphans—I will come to you. In just a little while the world will not see me again, but you will. For I will live again, and you will too" (John 14:15–20).

"I am leaving you with a gift—peace of mind and heart. And the peace I give isn't like the peace the world gives. So don't be troubled or afraid" (John 14:27).

1. Have you ever stood up for someone against the majority?
2. Have you ever misused your power?
3. Was it knowledge and wisdom beyond her years that made that little girl stand up against power? Or was it the Holy Spirit within her?
4. Were you taught racism is wrong by a parent or teacher when most people didn't think it wrong?
5. Can you think of a time when power was misused against you or someone you loved?

"Nearly all men can stand adversity, but if you want to test a man's character, give him power."—Abraham Lincoln

The Scriptures

Question: Do you think it is sinful to question anything in the Bible? Which version do you prefer?

There are many passages that I have problems with when I read the Bible, especially in the Old Testament; however, we are debating currently how we should deal with homosexuality, even though it is clearly stated in our scriptures to be sinful, in both the Old and New Testaments.

I think that we should keep in mind it is called the "Old Testament" for a reason. The "New Testament" I believe was meant to fulfill, clarify, expand, or correct the Old Testament. It is amazing that the general advice given about love is valid throughout the centuries. The New Testament, which was brought into being by the life and teachings of Jesus, brings love to the center of our very being and relationship with others and therefore with our God. As we live our lives, we can have happier and more fulfilled lives if we love ourselves and each other. When we do this, we love our God.

Jesus did not write anything down that we know of, and he spoke to just a few individuals as compared to the multitude of peoples and cultures that existed during his short life. His message of love has somehow spread around the world and through time, undiluted and just as powerful as it was in his small world and his time.

I have a set of books written by Robert G. Ingersoll, a philosopher, speaker, and agnostic of the nineteenth century. I recently picked one up and read a few chapters that he wrote about people he thought important in humankind's development of understanding. He wrote about Shakespeare, Voltaire, Abraham Lincoln, Walt Whitman, and others he thought deserved our attention. Ingersoll also had a chapter on the Bible. I had some difficulty disagreeing with some of his thoughts. Most of his dissertation was about the Old Testament and the seeming irrationality of God's anger, jealousy, and vengeance, mostly in the two books of Kings. I agree that there were many books in the Old Testament that describe a God who reacts to earthly things in a human way. We all try to get God to conform to our will instead of attempting to conform to his will. We want to make God into our image. We Christians should understand that God is pure love; only one person ever lived who fully understood this and lived a life of pure love.

Some people think the US Constitution should be a living document, one that should be interpreted and changed as society evolves. Others think that the mechanism provided for change was flawed and should be circumvented. Our Bible consists of scriptures that were written over centuries, sometimes by unknown authors. The bishops of our early Christian church convened at the Council of Carthage in 397 A.D. with the purpose of putting the imprimatur of the church upon certain scriptures and eliminating others. During the Reformation, the Bible was changed somewhat in its content; there are various versions today. There was never a format or mechanism provided for the Bible to be a so-called living document like the US Constitution. There are some inconsistences in our scriptures that trouble some people; they want to want to discard the whole because of them. I've been able to avoid this by keeping in mind the simple concept of love that Jesus taught. If God wanted these scriptures to be written without flaws, he could have created them in a language understandable by all. God has chosen in his wisdom to speak to us through our own minds and to guide those thoughts by the truth of Jesus's life and the Holy Spirit.

The simple truth is to love each other and to therefore love God. We can choose to find fault with some of the Bible and even discard the whole thing as a bunch of foolishness, as Ingersoll did. We've been given freedom to learn how to love. We've been given freedom to think whatever we want as we live our lives. This is how God wants us to learn, and it is the only reason we are given this life: to learn how to love. Ingersoll failed to see that the purpose for humankind was to learn to love. He thought that our purpose was to develop freedom of thought, which he found confining in a Christian mentality. He failed to see the total freedom provided by a loving God. The failure of the Christian church to continually exist through the centuries and grow in the love of Christ does not invalidate it. My personal belief is that looking for things to invalidate the message of love brought by Christ is futile and fruitless. Any imprimatur that claims the message of love in scripture is from God is good. We are encouraged to pray for the guidance of the Holy Spirit as our imprimatur.

Power from the Holy Spirit is not limited to strength beyond the ordinary. That power also involves courage, boldness, confidence, insight, ability, and authority.

"But when the Holy Spirit has come upon you, you will receive power and will tell people about me everywhere—in Jerusalem, throughout Judea, in Samaria, and to the ends of the earth" (Acts 1:8).

"But now that faith in Christ has come we no longer need the law as our Guardian" (Galatians 3:24).

1. Have you ever questioned anything in your Bible?
2. Who do you think decided upon what scriptures to put in the Bible?
3. Do you believe the Bible to be the complete word of God?
4. Translations of the earlier scriptures varied, such as describing Mary as "a young woman" in some and as "a virgin" in others. Do these variances matter?
5. Are you afraid to ask the Holy Spirit to take over your spiritual essence?
6. If you want to look for it, you can find evil deeds in the Bible. Ingersoll probably knew much about the content of the Bible but sought inconsistencies instead of God's love. Can there be human error in the Bible?
7. Can we answer questions that bother us through wisdom from the Holy Spirit and Jesus as well as scriptures?

The Spirit of Christmas: Christmas Past, Christmas Present, and Christmas Yet-to-Come

Question: What have you learned from Christmas past to make this Christmas one to remember in the future?

Many years ago, an older man was leaving my pharmacy the day before Christmas and I said to him, "I hope you have a Merry Christmas!"

The likeable gentleman turned and said, "Christmas is just another day to my wife and me. We don't have children, so it will be just like any other day."

They've both been gone for years now, and I regret that I didn't try to make their Christmas a joyful experience. A few years ago, I remembered this failure and invited an old gentleman who had recently lost his wife to come to our home for Christmas celebration. I was surprised by his immediate acceptance. I soon found that he was a friend of my father-in-law, who was also coming to our home with my mother-in-law. That Christmas dinner was one that will always be remembered because this gentleman, my in-laws, and a brother-in-law passed from this life just a few years later. The Christmas pictures show the smiling faces of these four enjoying a wonderful dinner and the love felt on a special day honoring Christ's birth. I often wish that I had invited the childless couple to come to our home sooner and enjoy our children as they brought the Christmas spirit to all of us. Jesus taught us that unless we have their kind of faith, we will never get into the Kingdom of God. We need their simple understanding of love to understand the spirit of Christmas.

For most, but not all, Christians, few experiences fill us with more love for others and the life God has given us than the experience of Christmastime. It's because most of us become like little children and remember past joys while trying to recreate them. Christmas can be a time of bittersweet memories as we get older because we all have lost loved ones and miss their physical presence. It is a time when a fragrance of a peeled orange or a real Christmas tree flushes warm memories of Christmas past from their hiding places in our hearts. It is a time when hearing a carol will bring the smiling faces of loved ones to life in our minds, even though they are in Jesus's presence now. It is a good thing to let tears roll down our cheek with a smile on our lips to taste the memories they bring. Just as we hold the spirit of Jesus by the Holy Spirit's presence in us, we hold a spiritual presence of those gone on to add love to our celebration.

Some struggling Christians ask too many questions and let their intellect and their emotions get in the way. Their darkness will not let them see the real joy of Christmas. That is why we are told by Jesus, "I have come as a light to shine in this dark world, so that those who put their trust in me will no longer remain in the darkness" (John 12:45–46).

Each Christmas, I take a little time alone to toast my friends and family who have gone to be with Jesus. An old friend and I did this together for a few years by taking another sip from a bottle a friend shared with each of us before he died. I notice there is only a sip left for me to share those memories alone this year. I will let the warmth of this last sip remind me of the heartwarming friendships I have had and remind me to continue to build new relationships today for tomorrow's celebrations.

When I was a child, our little church always had a Christmas program the week before Christmas. There would be a large cedar tree in the corner, filling the church with its fragrance. On the night of the program, little children would parade one at a time to stand before the congregation and recite a piece from memory (often needing help from an adult in the front row). The pride we felt when we finished was our reward. As we became a little older, we would become wise men and shepherds with bathrobes, towels, and Grandma's cane. Later in the evening, there would be a visit by old Santa, bursting through the door with gifts of Christmas candy and oranges. Old Santa reminded us of Earl Smoot as he yelled, "Merry Christmas," on his exit, but his magic worked because childlike faith filled everyone's heart. One year, he lost his hat as he ran from the churchyard and my older brother found it. As he held it in his hand, it was like the Holy Grail. He had to give it up, but for a moment, he actually held this sacred object in his hands. I can still see his eyes sparkle as they stared off into some magical place.

Several years ago, an old school buddy called and asked if I would be interested in going to our old church, where the Christmas program was still being held. I excitedly replied yes; it just happened that my brother was going to be visiting at that time. We had a wonderful evening that seemed to pull us into another time. Everything was the same as decades ago. The only things missing were Earl Smoot as Santa, and a real cedar tree.

Today, if I pinch a cedar leaf and hold it to my nose, I am filled with the warmth of those wonderful days. There also was the combined fragrance of those hard Christmas candies as we each searched for our favorite. I always looked for cinnamon candy but often chose the wrong one. When I peel an orange with a grandchild today, I hold it close to their nose and say, "It smells like Christmas." This always brings a smile, and I hope it makes a memory.

"One day some parents brought their children to Jesus so he could touch them and bless them, but the disciples told them not to bother him. But when Jesus saw what was happening, he was very displeased with his disciples. He said to them, 'Let the children come to me. Don't stop them! For the Kingdom of God belongs to such as these. I assure you, anyone who doesn't have their kind of faith will never get into the Kingdom of God.' Then he took the children into his arms and placed his hands on their heads and blessed them" (Mark 10:13–16).

1. In order to feel the Christmas spirit, don't we have to become children again at Christmas?
2. Some people have had unpleasant Christmas experiences because of evil. What can you do to make this a happy Christmas for these people?
3. Have you ever heard someone say, "I will be glad when Christmas is over"? What are they missing?
4. What can you do to make Christmas a little more enjoyable for your spouse?
5. Have you ever had to spend Christmas away from loved ones? Did you surround yourself with thoughts of Christmas past? Did you seek someone else having the same experience and share Christmas love with them?
6. If you've had bad experiences in Christmas past, what's keeping you from making this Christmas a wonderful one?

The Trinity

Question: Do you think one of the Trinity is more important than the other two, or are they the same? (Ephesians 4:4–7).

I often use the analogy of a three-legged stool when explaining life to younger people. I tell them that they are like a three-legged stool; they are made up of a mind, body, and soul. They should understand that each leg is as important as the other, and each leg needs constant nourishing, or they will eventually fall on their rear. All parts support the whole and are a part of the wholeness of a human.

I recently thought about how the Trinity is the ultimate example of our understanding of the value of our three parts. Consider the mind being our Father God, and the body being Jesus, the Father made flesh, and the Holy Spirit being the soul of our blessed Trinity, which is present in each human. The Holy Spirit is the tie that binds each of us to the Father and Son. The difference is that the legs of the Trinity feed us instead of us feeding our mind, body, and soul. It is our choice to accept that food from God or not. That acceptance is the choice that makes us whole. It opens the circuit that makes us whole in his sight. If we do not let the Holy Spirit feed our mind, body, and soul, we will not be connected to the Father and Son. The circuit, as in electricity, will not be complete. We will fall if we do not accept that connection to our God through his Son and the Spirit that fills and binds us all.

Muslims are taught by the Quran that "unbelievers are those that say God is one of three; there is but one God" (5:73). There is but one God; however, this one God has chosen to be manifested in three ways. He has the power and wisdom to do this. The Quran states God is only one God (4:171).

"Those who say, God is the Messiah, the son of Mary are defying the truth" (5:17). "The Messiah, son of Mary, was no other than a messenger" (5:75). "The Christians say that the Messiah is the son of Allah; may Allah destroy them" (9:30). It is true that Christianity and Islam share some things in common. But what they do not share is a fundamental understanding of who God is and what he is like.

We Christians believe that God became human through Jesus so that we would understand that he could endure the pain and suffering of this world and not lose the fundamental principle of love, through his sacrifice for our sins. God sent his Holy Spirit to give all who would accept his presence the strength to endure with the same love in this world. By faith, we can appropriate the Holy Spirit's power each day. Jesus told us that the world at large would not recognize the Holy Spirit.

Ash Wednesday is the beginning of the celebration of the passion of our Lord Jesus. During these forty days, we should remind ourselves that God offered his Son as a sacrifice for our sins. The suffering we sometimes endure in this life will be made easier by the presence of the Holy Spirit sent by God, which completed the Trinity. It's the third leg of our support system.

"If you love me, obey my commandments. And I will ask the Father and he will give you another Counselor who will never leave you. He is the Holy Spirit, who leads into all truth. The world at large cannot receive him because it isn't looking for him and doesn't recognize him. But you do, because he lives with you now and later will be in you" (John 14:17).

1. Do you believe you have the Holy Spirit? What can you do to become aware of his presence?
2. Do we receive the Holy Spirit when we are baptized?
3. Do you believe the Holy Spirit helps us understand if we call upon him?
4. Can we use the Holy Spirit, God, and Jesus interchangeably?

5. Is accepting and receiving the Holy Spirit different from accepting Jesus?
6. Is laying on of hands necessary to receive the Holy Spirit? Is this only a symbolic act?
7. Didn't Jesus detest the symbolism utilized by the Jewish leaders?

The Twilight Zone

Question: Was there anything you dreamed about but thought would never happen but did?

I've spent a lot of time in my life daydreaming. When I was about five years old, I remember lying in a field by my house, watching a yellow Piper Cub airplane flying overhead and dreaming of being a pilot. I used to turn a footstool upside down in the living room and imagine it to be an airplane; I would fly it around like I had seen the yellow Cub. I was also convinced that I could fly like Superman if I wore the proper cape and had enough confidence. Unfortunately, I never got my footstool off the ground; I never had quite enough confidence to leap into the air and glide as I had dreamed I could. Even today, I still dream that I can fly by stretching my arms then glide as far as I want. The minute my confidence wanes in my dream, I come back to the ground. The feeling of being able to fly in my dream is exuberating.

Sometimes, parents scold children for daydreaming; we are told that "an idle mind is the devil's workshop." We also may tell them that their nighttime dreams are only dreams and have no relation to reality. I think daydreaming should be encouraged with adult guidance, and night dreams should be interpreted with kind understanding. Albert Einstein said that some of his best ideas came from "something like daydreaming." That area sometimes called the twilight zone is a creative thinking area somewhere between consciousness and sleep. This is an area where we shut out the noise of our environment and allow our mind to flow freely. Not only can we solve many problems by this method, but we can create pathways to creativeness we may think we are incapable of achieving.

We can build a positive pathway for our venture into the twilight zone by mentally drawing an outline, which our subconscious will utilize with practice. When Lewis Carroll sat down to write *The Adventures of Alice in Wonderland*, I wonder if he expected his mental adventure would produce the many lessons about life that resulted. Our minds are capable of so much more than we realize, if we allow the freedom of thoughts in a positive area. We should also keep in mind that if allowed, our minds can lead us to sin and destructiveness if not disciplined and coaxed to wholesome areas. The most powerful sex organ we have is our brain, and our sexual activity would not be as pleasurable without allowing those sexual thoughts. We should be aware that total freedom of sexual thoughts can and may lead to misdeeds and destructive behavior. Jesus cautioned us that we may sin if we even think about adultery because he knew that thoughts lead to behavior and action.

There must be an understanding that we cannot always keep our minds from wandering into areas that might allow misconduct, but we should avoid allowing habits or going to those areas that may lead us astray. People who preach total avoidance of these kinds of thoughts can even do great harm to young minds.

With the increase and availability of pornography, young as well as older minds can be led to undesirable actions, but restricting young minds sometimes creates more curiosity. The electronic games available for our youth today may lead some undisciplined minds to destructive behavior in real life.

Judgmental adults have tried to ingrain in us thoughts that we are not allowed. We are not allowed to have sexual thoughts, we are not allowed to masturbate, we are not allowed to consider any religion except one, we can only believe one political party. We can allow all these rules to be adopted at some point in our life, or we can sort through them with the wisdom and education we achieve to find the rules that make sense. Dr. Wayne Dyer suggests in his book, *You'll See It When You Believe It*, to "look at any and all beliefs that you carry around with you in terms of how well they serve you in living a life of harmony and purpose." He also advises the more you are at ease with the behavior of others, even if you do not act that way yourself, the more you are at ease with yourself.

The more we are at ease with ourselves, the more we are able to forgive ourselves. When we are able to forgive (not excuse, which attempts to lessen the blame) ourselves, we are accepting God's forgiveness.

Allow yourself and your children to enjoy the joy and freedom of daydreaming. Allow those creative juices to be released from controls placed there by others, but keep your own guideposts visible to that creative mind as you travel into the twilight zone.

"There is so much more we would like to say about this. But you don't seem to listen, so it's hard to make you understand. You have been Christians a long time now, and you ought to be teaching others. Instead you need someone to teach you again the basic things a beginner must learn about the Scriptures. You are like babies who drink only milk and cannot eat solid food, and a person who is living on milk isn't very far along in the Christian life, and doesn't know much about doing what is right. Solid food is for those who are mature, who have trained themselves to recognize the difference between right and wrong and then do what is right" (Hebrews 5:11–14).

"We should live in this evil world with self-control, right conduct, and devotion to God" (Titus 2:12).

"Now, why should my freedom be limited by what someone else thinks? If I can thank God for the food and enjoy it, why should I be condemned for eating it? Whatever you eat or drink or whatever you do, you must do all for the glory of God" (1 Corinthians 10:29–31).

1. Is Paul trying to teach us about discernment that we must train our conscience, our senses, our mind, and our body to distinguish between good and evil?
2. Do you think that we sometimes want God's banquet before we are capable of digesting it?

3. If you allow your mind to travel into the twilight zone, are we as Christians to allow no restrictions?
4. If we don't question what others think, how can we grow as humans?
5. Is it okay for us to question all rules?

"There is nothing like a dream to create the future."—Victor Hugo

To Thine Own Self Be True

Question: What do you think this quote means? Did your parents ever say something similar?

Many people are aware of this quote. Some think it's from the Bible; however, it is from Shakespeare's play, *Hamlet*. The Danish Lord Polonius is a man, like a lot of us fathers, who likes to preach to his son. He is perhaps absorbed by the sound of his own voice. The son is getting ready to leave for Paris, and ol' Dad is rattling off lots of advice, like be careful who you hang around with, and so on. The advice most of us remember is that it's important to know yourself and remember how you are raised. If you can't be honest with yourself, you can't be honest with others.

I wonder if many of us are totally honest with ourselves. We like to think we are, and in the process, we like to say things like, "I'm the type of person …" (you fill in the rest of the sentence). We try to describe ourselves to others to justify our failures. You never hear anyone say, "I'm the type of person who will do anything—lie, cheat, or steal—to get ahead in life." Many of us are afraid to completely examine who we are. We also are dishonest with ourselves when we try to understand how we became who we are. Perhaps we think our financial successes were planned and executed to create a better life, when it really was to prove to our parents that we were more valuable than they thought. On the opposite end, we may have deliberately failed to prove to someone, perhaps ourselves, that we *are* worthless.

Some people never look at themselves and go through life pretending to be something other than what they are, like an actor in a role. The Bible says, "Thou shalt not bear false witness." This means not to lie to others or ourselves. A lie is coward's way of getting out of trouble, and when we begin by lying to ourselves, we're soon lying to others. Dishonest people soon begin to believe the lies they construct around themselves. They lose the ability to tell the difference between truth and lies. By believing your own lies, you deceive yourself, you alienate yourself from God, and you lose credibility in all your relationships. In the long run, honesty wins out. A few white lies, and we soon become color blind. It isn't long after we move the line of truthfulness a few times and we forget where the original line was, but God will remember.

During an election, people examine the candidates, who go on endlessly, trying to convince us they possess the virtues they think most people want. We the people either believe they're being honest or we don't. News people will sometimes amplify those virtues or detract from them in efforts to inform or misinform. Honesty seems to become pliable in politics. If we are honest with ourselves, we will understand honesty is pliable with most people, including old number one. An example might be, "I will keep what you just told me a secret." After making this pledge, we tell our spouse or best friend, "Now, don't tell anyone, but I was just told …" Afterward, we try to excuse the breach of promise, saying, "I can keep a secret but the ones I tell can't."

Most of us understand that a little dishonesty has its place in social decorum. Ladies cannot tell each other that they think their hair looks like it was done up by a five-year-old with a pair of dull scissors and a can of spray paint. We cannot say to our pastor as we leave church on Sunday that he is full of BS. Sometimes, it is best to remain quiet, remembering, "I am the master of my unspoken word, and a slave to those that should have remained unspoken."

We are responsible for our own destiny, while knowing we all fall short of understanding true love and honesty. We are imperfect, but if we seek a better self through Christ, we should be unafraid of the unknown because God's grace and the sacrifice made by Jesus on the cross pay the price for sins. We can be undefeated by trials of this life and not be fearful of the unknown of the next.

"Well then, if you teach others, why don't you teach yourself? You tell others not to steal, but do you steal? You say it is wrong to commit adultery, but do you do it? You condemn idolatry, but do you steal from pagan temples? You are so proud of knowing the law, but you dishonor God by breaking it. No wonder the Scriptures say, 'The world blasphemes the name of God because of you'" (Romans 2:21–24).

"Anyone who listens to my teaching and obeys me is wise, like a person who builds a house on solid rock. Though the rain comes in torrents and the floodwaters rise and the winds beat against that house, it won't collapse, because it is built on rock. But anyone who hears my teaching and ignores it is foolish, like a person who builds a house on sand. When the rains and floods come and the winds beat against that house, it will fall with a mighty crash" (Matthew 7:24–27).

"Blessed are those who wash their robes. They will be permitted to enter through the gates of the city and eat the fruit from the tree of life. Outside the city are the dogs—the sorcerers, the sexually immoral, the murderers, the idol worshipers, and all who love to live a lie" (Revelation 22:14–15).

1. Have you ever told a little lie to avoid a social commitment? Do you sometimes tell little lies because it's convenient?
2. Have you ever let an untruth that elevates you in the eyes of others stand?
3. Have you ever tried to live someone else's life?
4. Have you ever blamed others for your bad choices?
5. Can you admit that you make many bad choices that may harm others?
6. Have you ever felt beaten by life's slings and arrows, then want to create a lie to become elevated?
7. Do you ever lie to yourself about your talents to avoid serving God?
8. Have you ever feared being found out?

Invictus

Out of the night that covers me,
Black as the Pit from pole to pole,
I thank whatever gods may be
For my unconquerable soul.
In the fell clutch of circumstance
I have not winced nor cried aloud.
Under the bludgeonings of chance
My head is bloody, but unbowed.
Beyond this place of wrath and tears
Looms but the horror of the shade,
And yet the menace of the years
Finds, and shall find, me unafraid.
It matters not how strait the gate,
How charged with punishments the scroll,
I am the master of my fate; I am the captain of my soul.
William Ernest Henley (1849–1903)

Trust and Faith

Question: Do you ever fail to trust God? Were you impatient with him?

Our physical bodies are made up of millions and millions of cells. Each cell in our body contains our book of life, our genetic instructions (except blood cells, which contain no nucleus). Most of us have studied this to some extent in school and forgot or never understood it from the beginning. But the short answer is that each cell has a nucleus that contains chromosomes made up of genes that are made up of long strands of DNA. We all have twenty-three pairs of chromosomes: twenty-three from Mom and twenty-three from Dad. Males have X and Y chromosomes, and females have two X chromosomes. These X and Y chromosomes are what determines if we are male or female (makes you wonder about the controversy in our political world about what a male and a female is).

When we mate and produce a child, we trust our book of life to produce a healthy baby, while we have faith in the system created for reproduction. I cannot understand how people can think this faith in the system of creating a child is anything other than faith in God. Faith is a noun that requires no evidence for belief, other than the obvious. Trusting is a verb requiring some actions. That is why trust is the necessary foundation of love. Trust is earned; it is created.

The design of the system for life in the universe was from the God of everything. This God is the universe seen and unseen. This God is complete knowledge, complete trustworthiness, and complete love. This complete trustworthiness was manifested in our world by the presence of Christ. This Christ is worthy of our complete love. We cannot love him, however, if we do not trust him. This is true in human relationships, as well. We cannot love each other without trust. We should not give up on someone because they were once untrustworthy. We would ask for the same treatment from others, just as Christ never gives up on us.

I have read of a new DNA editing technique developed by scientists at USC Berkley, which can be utilized to change the strands of DNA. I have faith that science can discover and even alter aberrant gene expression, but I don't trust humans to always use this ability in good ways. If they can alter genes in the anopheles mosquitoes, which spread malaria, by making them sterile, someone could perhaps do the same in humans. Will the bad possibilities outweigh the ability to eliminate sickle-cell disease and other genetic diseases like breast cancer? The developments in biotechnology are outpacing our ability to predict the outcome.

Each of us has a responsibility to listen to our God when he speaks to us in various ways. We are to utilize our God-given abilities, have faith in God's presence in our lives, and trust him to guide us to make this world a better place. My daughter just attended a small conference this past weekend with the author of the novel *The Shack*, who believes God wrote the book through him. The book has sold millions and changed atheists into believers. What if he had not listened to God's encouragement?

A man from St. Louis called me recently to tell me he had read my book, *Questions*, and that it had made a difference in his life. I was driving down a crooked road, so I pulled off into a church parking lot. As I sat there, talking to this man, the person who inspired me to write the book pulled up beside me, with a smile on his face. Was God trying to tell me something? Perhaps it is to trust his guidance when I write and not ignore his little messages. Each of us has unique abilities that God can utilize for his glory; therefore, we should all pay attention when God sends us message in different ways. God has chosen to utilize us as his voice; therefore, when we ignore his messages, we quiet his voice. We must listen and trust his wisdom. We must have faith that God speaks to each of us and wants to speak through each of us. We are all unique because of our genetic makeup; we are all a small note in God's symphony. Let us have faith that God wrote that music and trust that our small note will make a positive difference. We can choose to be a part of God's beautiful music or be a sour note, like an aberrant gene in a damaged chromosome.

"Unless you are faithful in small matters, you won't be faithful in large ones. If you cheat even a little, you won't be honest with greater responsibilities. And if you are untrustworthy about worldly wealth, who will trust you with the true riches of heaven? And if you are not faithful with other people's money, why should you be trusted with money of your own?" (Luke 16:10–12).

"What is faith? It is the confident assurance that what we hope for is going to happen. It is the evidence of things we cannot yet see. God gave his approval to people in days of old because of their faith.

"By faith we understand that the entire universe was formed at God's command, that what we now see did not come from anything that can be seen" (Hebrews 11:1).

1. Have you been ignoring God's messages to you?
2. Do you trust completely in Jesus, or do you want to give him instructions?
3. Do you have patience enough to let God work in your life, or do you think God is not listening to you?
4. If you could go back in time and clip out the bad parts, would you do it, or would you be afraid that the present would be altered in a negative way?
5. Have you asked God to use your small talents without reservations?
6. Do you think the bad parts of your life made you a better person today?

Unraveling Government, Politics, Religion, and Life

Question: Is it possible today to talk about life without involving government, politics, and religion? And is it possible to do this without rancor? Should we have a Bible study without ever discussing current events, because of factions?

It is my belief that we cannot and should not unravel Christianity from our government, and factions are necessary for some truths to emerge, within religion, politics, and government.

The Declaration of Independence outlined our founding fathers' moral vision and the government it embodied. It stated, "We hold these truths to be self-evident," which invokes the tradition that there is a higher law of right and wrong from which to derive human law. These moral truths are that "all men are created equal, that they are endowed by their Creator with certain unalienable rights that among these are life, liberty, and the pursuit of happiness. That to secure these rights, governments are instituted among men, deriving their just powers from the consent of the governed."

The Constitution of the United States of America was written to define our new system of governing and the balance of powers between the described three branches of government. Our original Constitution allowed for amendments, and the first amendment stated that Congress shall make no law respecting an *establishment* of religion or prohibiting the free exercise thereof or abridging the freedom of speech, or of the press, or the right of the people *peaceably* to assemble, and to petition the government for a redress of grievances. This amendment and the next nine are known as the

Bill of Rights. They basically protect the people from government's excess use of power over our individual lives.

The Federalist Papers were a series of eighty-five essays written to promote the ratification of the Constitution. They are not part of the Constitution but attempt to explain it, and even today, they are used to explain our Constitution. Some of these essays describe limits of governing powers and the dangers that may arise if the Constitution was not ratified. In Federalist Paper No. 2, John Jay talked with pleasure about how the people in the newly established country came from the same area, spoke the same language, and had the same religion.

Just as our Constitution was not perfect, we the people are not perfect in our interpretation. We are advised by the Federalist papers to continue to be informed in order to promote better government. We often are divided in our opinions, and in our efforts to understand our system of government, we use political methods to persuade the people that our understanding is better than theirs. The nature of politics is to overstate things in a manner that will develop followers. By failing to remain informed, even to the point of failing to teach government in our schools, we may be swayed in undesired directions. Some factions want us to believe that the First Amendment provides for the freedom from religion, instead of providing for free exercise thereof. It simply states that the government shall not establish any one religion for the entire country, but we are free to follow any religion. I believe that the founding fathers did not mean that to include any ideology that had a primary purpose of destroying our method of government through a process that is a core element of what some would present as a religion.

While many today want to deny it as a fact, our founding fathers were influenced by a belief in a Supreme Being and the ethical principles described by Judeo-Christian scriptures. Other countries around the world have established their governments utilizing different principles. Some cultures deny women certain rights, according to a different set of moral principles. The rights of minorities are denied to the point of making some religions illegal. It took many years before our own government provided equal rights for all people. We have not always understood our governing principles perfectly but are in the process of establishing a more perfect union.

We cannot unravel the intertwining of Judeo-Christian principles, which inform our system of government, without destroying its very nature and essence. Some factions have that as their ultimate goal. They've learned how to achieve this by exploiting the freedoms established by the very Constitution they oppose. No society can be completely free because that would be anarchy. No society can survive without some established restrictions on some freedoms.

During times of social turmoil or world conflict, the people's rights and freedoms are necessarily modified by the legislative body so that we can be protected from danger coming from outside or within our country. Unfortunately, those who mean to do us harm utilize our desire to protect rights and freedoms to their advantage.

Christians believe God allows us to be free to believe whatever we want to believe. This comes at some possible peril, however. We believe that any government not established under the Christian principle of love is a flawed government. It is impossible to unravel this basic principle from our government because it is the basic informer of our government. As Christians, we desire that the noise of political conversation be governed by truth and tolerance. We understand that we cannot converse without danger of antipathy; however, this should not dissuade us from understanding the necessary intertwining of the principles of our faith with our government and our lives.

The basic rights of our Constitution do not apply to those who are not citizens. We utilize common sense most often, but not always, to understand this. This common sense informs us that these rights will be granted to anyone who lawfully becomes a citizen and subscribes to the tenets of our Constitution and laws provided under it.

As believers in a supreme being, we should understand that there was a moral calling for a place on earth to be established where the God-given rights of people would be protected. I pray we hold this to be self-evident and work to preserve this bastion of freedom.

There are false teachers of our Constitution who want to unravel Christian principles from our government and daily lives by continuously presenting ideas that are not constitutional. There are also false teachers about our Christian faith who present ideas that are not biblical, until many begin to believe them. There are many false teachers waiting to destroy your Christ-centered life.

Jesus said, "Render unto Caesar the things that are Caesar's and unto God the things that are God's,"{Matt 22:21}, meaning there are certain functions necessarily performed by government, but God is overall master. The philosophy of Christianity is that we are here on earth to learn about love, and this is best learned freely by individuals with counsel from parents and teachers. Love of others and religion are not to be forced by the government. We differ in that aspect from Islam, which has the ideology from Muhammad that Islam is an entire religious-political-legal system. Christianity allows us to believe or not. Islam calls for barbaric punishments under Sharia law, which is embraced by a large number of Muslims. Islam is not a religion in our Western sense of the word. Islam does not blend with our Constitution, just as Communism does not blend with freedom promoted by our Declaration of Independence.

Our country as well as practicing Christians in spite of all the information available have become undereducated and poorly informed. We know a little about a lot of things, but this makes it difficult for us to know whether we know what we're talking about or not. And when we do not know or do not know enough, we tend to substitute emotions for thoughts. This deepens divisions and make Christians and Americans vulnerable to false teachers and loss of our values.

"But you, my dear friends, must remember what the apostles of our Lord Jesus Christ told you, that in the last times there would be scoffers whose purpose in life is to enjoy themselves in every evil way imaginable. Now they are here, and they are the ones who are creating divisions among you.

They live by natural instinct because they do not have God's Spirit living in them" (Jude 1:17–19).

"What is causing the quarrels and fights among you? Isn't it the whole army of evil desires at war within you? You want what you don't have, so you scheme and kill to get it. You are jealous for what others have, and you can't possess it, so you fight and quarrel to take it away from them. And yet the reason you don't have what you want is that you don't ask God for it. And even when you do ask, you don't get it because your whole motive is wrong—you want only what will give you pleasure" (James 4:1–3).

1. Do you believe Sharia law can (or should) coexist with the US Constitution?
2. If someone does not agree with a federal law, can they disobey it without consequences?
3. Should the Bible be allowed to be amended like our Constitution was?
4. Do some people scoff at you because you believe the Bible teaches certain behaviors are sinful?
5. Do you ever scoff at people who disagree with you? Isn't that what causes rancor?
6. Do you believe Christian principles should be removed from our governing philosophy?
7. Is it harmful to faith to have different understanding of scriptures? Or is it helpful to strengthen faith?

"There are again two methods of removing the causes of faction: the one, by destroying liberty which is essential to its existence, the other, by giving to every citizen the same opinions, the same passions, and the same interests."—James Madison, Federalist Paper No. 10

What a Good Boy Am I (I'm a Better Christian than You)

Question: Can you think of someone who influenced your Christian development in a positive or negative way?

As I approach the end of my life, I become more aware of the people who were in it. I bumped into many along the way without much notice, and then there were those who had a profound influence on me and how I lived my life. All of us have the same experience to varying degrees. Some of us are so into ourselves that we seldom give thought, much less credit, for their efforts and influences that shaped our way of living. I doubt there is one among us, though, who will not at times remember something a parent said or did that made us what we've become. Sometimes, what we've become because of those influences is not what our Lord Jesus would have desired. Each of us should examine the way we are living on a continual basis and try to understand and remember positive and negative influences that shaped us. Unfortunately, some people were raised by a parent or someone else who was impaired. It may have been drugs, alcohol, sexual deviation, or other sinful natures that made them harm our Christian development. We can and should examine these negative influences and put them in the open so that we can get beyond them in our future. The positive influences from parents, caregivers, and friends will hopefully be recognized and utilized for Christian growth.

There are those who watch each of us as we go about our business each day. It's important to be aware of being watched and perhaps being an example for someone to follow. Christians should take their mentorship seriously and make efforts to present a positive image in a humble manner, without the need for earthly adoration and reward. We all have a demon on our shoulder, whispering how good we are by our deeds. We will already be rewarded in an earthly fashion when we listen to that demon. We sometimes do those things Jesus wants us to do for others and keep secret, while thinking how good we are by doing these wonderful things, even keeping it a secret. Our pride has a strong pull. God would have us live a charitable life that becomes so much of who we are that we don't even think of adoration and reward. That is the goal for each Christian. As I write this, I personally ask God for his influence; I don't seek praise for his words. Like most people, I enjoy praise for my work, but I ask God to help me temper that feeling with true humility.

In Roman times, when a general returned in triumph parading through the streets with his bounty, a slave would stand behind him, holding a laurel over his head while continually whispering in his ear, "*Sic transit gloria*" (Fame is fleeting). It would behoove each of us aspiring Christians to replace that demon resting on our shoulder, telling us how good we are, with an angel saying, "Fame is fleeting."

"It is never too late to be what you might have been."—George Eliot. Just because we failed to live up to certain standards in the past, it is not too late to make corrections. With God's Holy Spirit, we can become better Christians, living according to the example of Jesus, seeking to love others as we would love ourselves, without the need for praise. God will praise those worthy of praise.

"Take care! Don't do your good deeds publicly, to be admired, because then you will lose the reward from your Father in heaven. When you give a gift to someone in need, don't shout about it as the hypocrites do—blowing trumpets in the synagogues and streets to call attention to their acts of charity! I assure you, they have received all the reward they will ever get. But when you give to someone, don't tell your left hand what your right hand is doing. Give your gifts in secret, and your Father, who knows all secrets, will reward you" (Matthew 6:1–4).

1. What should we teach our children and grandchildren about praise and pride?
2. Do you think trophies and ribbons can strengthen children's self-worth?
3. Can you remember people who did kind things just because that's how they were?
4. What do you think of people who continually blow their own horns?
5. Are you ever embarrassed when someone praises you for an act of charity?
6. Do you ever grade someone else's Christianity?

What Can I Do

Question: Have you ever wanted to do something for God but didn't know quite what to do?

"Ask not what your country can do for you, ask what you can do for your country." These words were spoken by John F. Kennedy at his inaugural address. Ted Sorenson, his speechwriter, was credited with the words, but history tells us that they were said in some form by many people over the years. They may have originally come from the prayer of St. Francis of Assisi: "Ask not so much to be consoled as to console, not to be loved but to love." Whatever the origin, they are thought provoking words which should change many minds in a selfish world.

There was a young lady getting ready to give blood at the United Methodist Church blood drive last week, talking to her reluctant boyfriend. My wife as a volunteer listened as she admonished her boyfriend, who wanted to back out.

"You need to do *something* to help other people," she said as he dropped his gaze to the floor.

"Okay," he finally responded. "I'll do it."

Mary told me a friend who also heard this conversation said she was impressed by the young lady's maturity. "She will go places," my wife's friend asserted.

This mature young lady had learned early in life that we cannot just be takers and live full lives. If we claim to be Christians, we have to give so that others can improve their lives.

Unfortunately, our country has been producing more takers than producers lately. People have become too comfortable letting state programs support them without doing anything for others. One presidential candidate recently said you can't change hearts; you need laws to make people change. This seems to go with what we believe as Christians. The basic tenet of Christianity is that God will transform us into a new person if we let him, by changing the way we think.

When we become that new person by accepting Christ, we naturally will want to help others. We sometimes limit what we do for others because we think we have no talent. We think we're not good speakers, so we may be hesitant to speak out and try to improve the lives of others. We may be disabled and think we cannot do things for others. There are as many excuses as there are people, but all of us have some talent, some skill that can help other people, animals, or the environment. God does not want us to continue to take without giving back in some measure.

What Would You Like to Say to the Future World?

Question: How can your simple little life have a positive effect on the future world?

I am in the possession of a notebook filled with poetry and wisdom written about 150 years ago. The author was Franklin Pryor, an African American preacher. Franklin filled this book by writing in beautiful cursive over about twenty-five years. The poetry tells me that this was a humble and good man who was well educated and very wise. The general theme is how to live this life and anticipation of a continued life in heaven. It is interesting to me because he would be 230 years old this very day, July 28, and yet it could have been written yesterday. Franklin loved the Lord and understood this life is all about loving one another. At the end of his book, he wrote a poem about the fourteenth chapter of John, which tells us the way to heaven has been secured by Jesus, and he leaves us with the gift of peace of mind. Jesus comforts us and says that he's not leaving us but staying with us as the Holy Spirit, so that we will not be troubled or afraid.

The last pages of Franklin's book of homemade poetry, as he called it, were filled with his last will and testament; he wanted a simple funeral, with his remains placed in a box of plain boards an inch and one half thick, and a simple gravestone. He wanted his simple stone to be inscribed with the words, "Franklin Pryor left this mortal form with a bright hope of immortality and eternal life" and the day, month, and year of his death. He made the comment that a tall stone would lead people to think he was more important than he was in this life. This simple inscription summarized the feeling one gets by reading the complete book of poetry.

For his children, Franklin wrote the following:

What I Want

I want that my children should learn all things and hold fast that which is good.

I want that they should live in harmony with each other and all others as far as possible.

I want that they should be wise concerning good and simple concerning evil and avoid the least appearance of evil.

I want that they should look through the operation of nature and as far as possible comprehend the utility of all diversified objects and conditions.

I want that they should do to others as they would have others do to them and forgive others as they would wish to be forgiven.

I want that they should live up to the good example of their natural father, but be sure and avoid all his errors and imperfections.

Franklin Pryor would have us read the words of Jesus in John 14 and then reflect upon the importance of accepting the gift of the Holy Spirit in our hearts so that we will not fear the present or the future. We are told of the truth of the Trinity and the assurance of continued life with them if we trust and obey Christ.

"All those who love me will do what I say. My Father will love them, and we will come to them and live with them. Anyone who doesn't love me will not do what I say. And remember, my words are not my own. This message is from the Father who sent me. I am telling you these things now while I am still with you. But when the Father sends the Counselor as my representative—and by the Counselor I mean the Holy Spirit—He will teach you everything and will remind you of everything I myself have told you.

"I am leaving you with a gift—peace of mind and heart. And the peace I give isn't like the peace the world gives. So don't be troubled or afraid. Remember what I told you: I am going away, but I will come back to you again. If you really love me, you will be very happy for me, because now I can go to the Father, who is greater than I am. I have told you these things before they happen so that you will believe when they do happen" (John 14:23–29).

The final wishes of Franklin Pryor blend well with the wishes of Jesus. He wanted his children to learn all things through the Holy Spirit and hold fast to that which is good. To love and forgive one another as we would want others to love and forgive us. May you be walking in the presence of our Lord Jesus Christ, Franklin Pryor. Happy birthday.

1. What do you think Franklin Pryor meant when he wanted his children to "look through the operation of nature and as far as possible comprehend the utility of all diversified objects and conditions"?
2. Why do you think Franklin Pryor's writings have survived over 150 years?
3. Ulysses S. Grant was president when these words were penned, and the Holy Spirit is just as good a counselor today as he was then. Do you listen to that Spirit?
4. Sin, fear, uncertainty, doubt, and numerous other forces are at war within us. The peace of God moves into our hearts and lives to restrain these hostile forces and offer comfort in place of conflict. Jesus says he will give us that peace if we are willing to accept it from him.
5. Do you believe the Holy Spirit will teach and comfort you during times of doubt and anxiety?

When to Stand up and When to Shut Up

Question: Have you ever stood up, thinking you had backing, only to discover that you were standing alone?

We changed the CEO at the bank where I had served for a few years on the board of directors. I continued to serve many more years, but with a little more wisdom. Our new president made some changes that were causing grumbling among the board members, including me. One of the changes had been to cut our stipend by half, and the meetings were reduced to once a month. I had talked with other members who mentioned it cost them to come to the meetings because they took time off from their profession to attend. I had no full-time pharmacist; therefore, I had to hire a relief pharmacist for the days of meetings. I took it upon myself to bring this up at the end of one meeting, only to hear silence. I had expected the grumblers to back me up, but they all remained silent.

When I asked someone if it cost him to attend the meetings, he left me swinging in the wind. His response was, "I look upon my duties here in the same manner I looked upon my duties as a school board member. I expect the sacrifice."

I sat back down and remembered the advice of our previous president: "Always have your ducks in a row when bringing anything up at a board or committee meeting." This was a time I spoke up but should have remained quiet.

There was one time that I should have stood up when I remained quiet. We had just played a round of golf and were having drinks discussing our game when a couple of men having lunch in another room walked past our table to the end of the bar to order a drink. One of the men happened to be African American. One of the men in my group shocked me by exposing his naked racism and bigotry.

The man asked, "Who let this n----- in?"

It became quiet and seeing no response from the two men, my friend repeated his vile question. I just sat there as the two men got their drinks and retreated to their luncheon. I have always regretted my silence. I should have walked up to this man at the bar and introduced myself, maybe offered to buy his drink. I could have punched my former friend in the nose, but that would have brought more attention to the incident than the African American man desired.

It is too easy to go along with the crowd, getting caught up in actions that we know to be wrong. I am sure all of us have paid the consequences for going along with the gang. Unfortunately, we still find it easier at times not to take a stand and declare something to be wrong, hateful, or destructive because we are afraid of criticism.

We can get caught up in negativity that may seem innocent; however, it can become harmful if we allow it to continue or participate in the process. We may find it somewhat entertaining to complain about people or situations without offering something positive in response. When you complain, you make yourself into a victim; when you offer something positive, you are in your power. Constant complainers act like victims in every situation. Farmers have learned to complain about the weather, price of fuel, fertilizer, profits, and so on, just like those in other professions do. A few years ago, there was a farmer who came to my pharmacy to get medicine for his mother. I sometimes tried to bait this good man by asking a question about the weather, price of grain, or whatever, but he never uttered anything but something positive in return. He was not going to let negativity take the joy out of his life. We should learn from people like him and not get caught up in the negativity others want to surround themselves within. When the crowd is complaining about how hot it is, we may respond something like, "Yes, isn't it wonderful? It reminds me of those days of my youth when we swam in a creek to cool off. We had so much fun on those long summer days."

As the Corinthians awaited Paul, they were given advice that we all should follow today:

"Be on guard. Stand true to what you believe. Be courageous, be strong, and everything you do must be done with love" (1 Corinthians 16:13).

Paul also advised the Philippians about thinking positively:

"Fix your thoughts on what is true and honorable and right. Think about things that are pure and lovely and admirable. Think about things that are excellent and worthy of praise" (Philippians 4:8).

1. Do you ever find yourself waiting for a complainer to finish so that you can complain?
2. Are there times that you should wait to offer Christian advice instead of making a scene in a crowd?
3. Paul seldom complained, even when he was imprisoned. What gave him strength to be positive?
4. I doubt that the little girl who stood up against the racist teacher realized how profound her example would be. Standing up for Christian teachings may be difficult, but it may have a ripple effect through time.
5. Those of us who remember World War II remember the racism taught as propaganda to win the war. It caused the incarceration of thousands of innocent Japanese Americans. Was this right?
6. What is the best way to overcome racism in today's world? Are we not being encouraged to dislike people from Muslim countries?
7. Do you try to control your thoughts? Do you think our thoughts are who we really are?

As a man thinks within himself, so is he. Proverbs 23:7

Whose Fault Is It?

Question: Have you ever been blamed for something you did not do?

There are two moments shared by all in life: birth and death. The part between these moments is what we call living. The question we should ask ourselves is, how do I live this life? Unfortunately, many of us do not put as much thought into this question as we should. If we fail to develop our own ideas, we will live a life that someone else wants us to live. Dictatorships and despots have learned that they can better control a society that is misinformed. They control their educational institutions, the media, and any sources of information available to the masses. After receiving only information favorable to the regime, the citizens soon become like sheep and are directed anywhere the dictator desires. Our spiritual lives can be affected in the same manner. If we do not develop and nurture our faith, we are in danger of living a faithless life, which contemporary society considers a desirable lifestyle. The idle mind can truly be the devil's workshop.

One Sunday, Mary and I made a quick trip to Walmart before church; I waited in our car near the entrance for her return. I thought about all the people entering and leaving the store on a Sunday morning, dressed in clothing that indicated they had not been to church that morning. When Mary returned, I said that something like 40 percent of our population seldom thought about God. She questioned my statistics, and I responded that I had read something about the percentage of people without faith. Later, in our pastor's sermon, he mentioned the same general figures. He said 40 percent of the people seldom thought about God; another 40 percent occasionally thought about God and faith but didn't do much to develop their faith. Then there was perhaps 20 percent that consciously made efforts to feed their faith and were thereby elevated by God. Whatever the exact figures are, there are a substantial number of people today who make no effort to have God in their lives and don't think godly thoughts.

Later in our day, we discussed a young couple we know who have said they no longer believe in God. My comments were that the young lady had been led astray by her husband, who had been reading materials that denied the existence of a deity.

Mary responded, "We are in charge of our own faith. We cannot fix blame upon others for our lack of faith."

She talked of the importance of questioning our beliefs so that we can grow in faith. She said, "Perhaps the young lady will emerge after this process a stronger person of faith; the blame should not be assigned to the young man for her current attitude."

In our search for our own truth, most of us have rebelled at times against authority; some of us benefit from that rebellion, and others do not. The problem we have when we rebel against God is lost faith. We are reminded many times in our scriptures that faith is necessary for Christians. The reason faith is required is because of our finite ability to understand, even if all truths were revealed to us. Most of us cannot even understand Einstein's theory of general relativity, much less all of God's truths. God can be found by logical thinking along with faith if applied; however, many of us do not think logically when making decisions. We often think emotionally, making bad choices that lead us to bad results.

We Christians are encouraged to attend church not because of God's needs but because of our own needs. We need to fill our minds and thoughts with things that lead us to understand love. We are given this precious life in order to learn how to love; our churches are there to help us understand true love.

We are ultimately responsible for our own choices and should not try to blame others for our disbelief or failures in life. We should try to prepare our mind, body, and soul to face the dangers in this life as we learn to understand why love of others is how we love God.

It seems that our world today wants us to attach blame to someone, other than the people who behave badly. Many people say that the police are the bad guys, and some people want to kill policemen just because they're doing their jobs. Parents don't want to blame someone else for their children's bad behavior. Teachers are blamed when undisciplined students fail to learn. Our overweight nation is attaching blame to food manufactures for our own lack of self-discipline. We blame guns for the mass killings instead of an ideology that teaches that killing Jews and Christians will please Allah.

"So get rid of all malicious behavior and deceit. Don't just pretend to be good! Be done with hypocrisy and jealousy and backstabbing. You must crave pure spiritual milk so that you can grow into the fullness of your salvation. Cry out for this nourishment as a baby cries for milk. Now that you have had a taste of the Lord's kindness.

"And now God is building you, as living stones, into his spiritual temple. What's more, you are God's holy priests, who offer the spiritual sacrifices that please him because of Jesus Christ.

"As the scriptures express it:

"'I am placing a stone in Jerusalem, a chosen cornerstone, and anyone who believes in him will never be disappointed.' Yes, he is very precious to you who believe. But for those who reject him,

"'The stone that was rejected by the builders has now become the cornerstone.'

"And the Scriptures also say,

"'He is the stone that makes people stumble,

"The rock that will make them fall'" (1 Peter 2:1–8).

1. If Jesus is called "the stone that makes people stumble, the rock that will make them fall," is that because they reject him?
2. Do you believe another person can cause you to lose your faith, or are you responsible for your own faith?
3. Do you ever blame others for your bad behavior?
4. Is there anything Christians can do to change our seemingly upside down world?
5. Is it a good thing to question your faith?
6. Does the fact that you're reading this book give you hope that you're in the 20 percent that God will elevate?
7. If life keeps going wrong for you, and you aren't looking at yourself, then it will continue to go wrong. Stop blaming others for your bad decisions.

Whose Life Is It, Anyway?

Question: How do you feel about abortion, the death penalty, euthanasia, suicide, murder, and war? When do we have the right to take a life without sinning against God?

I just attended a service honoring a friend who took his own life. The service was attended by many people who cared deeply for him. Some of his friends and family tried to understand the problems he faced, even if they did not agree with his solution. A few years ago, my father-in-law chose to end his life because his doctor told him he had Alzheimer's disease and offered little hope. My friend in high school was born with cerebral palsy, which implied that he wouldn't be able to find a mate or lead a somewhat normal life. He chose to end his young life, perhaps thinking he had become a burden. My uncle survived World War II and the Battle of the Bulge. He then survived cancer and was suffering from heart disease when he finally took his own life, which was also a part of mine. I've known many people who chose abortion because it seemed to be the best option at the time. They could not imagine the blessings that child could have brought our world. I have read about executions that were carried out by the state, only to discover later the person was innocent of the crime. Dr. Jack Kevorkian was going around the country helping supposedly terminally ill people end their lives, but we find out that some of those he assisted were only depressed and could have been helped. Some of the people Dr. Death assisted were not really terminal.

There seem to be so many variables in each situation, but when making a hard decision about any of these life-and-death issues, I'm usually (but not always) on the side of life. None of us really understand the mental state of another person nor the problems they face. We don't know the uplifting messages they failed to receive to bolster their faith. Many people grow up in broken families and have been mistreated physically, mentally, sexually in their young lives and were probably not guided by loving parents. Right and wrong became confusing issues at an early age and may be difficult for them to sort out in time to make good decisions. Physicians are not perfect and sometimes fail to see life through a patient's eyes, thereby offering little help. Family members are often so busy with their own problems, they have little energy to help others in need. After a tragic death, we often think, *Why didn't I call them last week when I thought about it? Why didn't I go by to visit when I had a chance?*

A few years ago, I was disusing abortion with a friend who was on the other side of the argument; I told him that I did not agree with abortion as an option. He became aggressive and asked me if I wanted to adopt any of the unwanted fetuses. Seeing his anger developing, I backed off and let the subject die. These issues are such hot topics; they're difficult to discuss in social settings without rancor. The death penalty is viewed strongly by anyone who's had a loved one killed. Those of us who are against capital punishment may have a different attitude if it was more personal. Aren't we as Christians supposed to forgive someone who killed another? Are their lives unrepairable in God's eyes?

If you think about it, didn't Jesus decide to go to Jerusalem, where he knew he would suffer and die? Could this be considered a form of suicide? If we choose to let nature take its course and not request medical intervention, are we doing anything less holy than our Lord? If we are confronted by the turmoil life sometimes presents and have been weakened by disease or other influences, can we be forgiven for choosing to leave this life on our own terms?

Islam allows no attempt to understand Muhammad's words in a modern context; they threaten any such attempt with death. This is why the structure of Islam will not allow moderation to develop, whereas Judaism and Christianity have a hierarchy that can modify the interpretation of the laws, such as the rabbinical prohibition that banned the biblical practice of polygamy. Christianity allows understanding of situations which cry for interpretation of scriptures in a modern context. We no longer stone gay people or adulterers. Universally developing wisdom, though slow, is encouraged by Christians. Wisdom developed over the ages can and should understand that human experience is different for each person and different today than two thousand years ago. Life-and-death questions are allowed to be discussed in Christianity in an attempt to see decisions through other perspectives. However, even within our culture, there is a tendency by academics to censor talk at universities that does not fit a liberal sensitivity, even to the point of not allowing certain words to be used in certain contexts (think the "N-word" in Mark Twain's books). Those who are of the pro-life point of view are not allowed to speak at some liberal arts colleges, therefore belying the "liberal" modifier.

All of us face turmoil in the process of living. Some of us have a mind-set that leads us to try to settle turmoil more rapidly than others. We can all lead more secure lives with positive thinking about the boiling soup of life if we see turmoil as a way to develop the perfect soup. We should give it time by trusting in Jesus to support rationality, with less anxiety as life's soup cooks.

"Always be full of joy in the Lord. I say it again: rejoice! Let everyone see that you are considerate in all you do. Remember, the Lord is coming soon.

"Don't worry about anything; instead, pray about everything. Tell God what you need, and thank him for all he has done. If you do this, you will experience God's peace, which is far more wonderful than the human mind can understand. His peace will guard your hearts and minds as you live in Christ Jesus" (Philippians 4:4–9).

1. Do some Christians still think that people who take their own life will be condemned to hell?
2. What do you do when there are things that seem to be falling apart all around you? Do you pray, do you get angry, do you strike out at others and seek to blame them?
3. Have you ever thought that the world would be better off without your presence?

4. Have you ever thought that other people would be better off dead, either because they are suffering or because they have caused suffering?
5. Do you ever think that some people should not be allowed to have children?
6. Do you think that abortion is the best choice sometimes, under certain circumstances, or never?
7. Could you be an executioner? What do you think Jesus would say to you if you had your hand on the lever to drop a murderer through the scaffolding at the end of a rope?
8. Is swearing in the context it was used two thousand years ago the same as cussing, which may be bad taste but perhaps not sinful?

Why Be a Christian?

Question: Why do you think being a Christian is the best way of life?

A few years ago, a friend asked me to write something about love. He said he wasn't sure he knew what it was. I wrote about a day I spent alone with my dad when I was about four years old. I believe that love is what Christianity is, and you can only teach about love by telling stories of love in action. Jesus often taught by using parables, and I have found this method to be the best way to help people understand.

If you substitute the word *love* for *Christianity,* it will be easier to understand why Christianity is the best way of life. Trust is the basic tenet for love to exist. Newborn babies already have the ability to trust when they come into this world. A new baby is totally dependent, and dependence requires trust. Fortunately, most learn to trust and love as they earn their independence. As newborns are fed and cared for, they learn to love their caregiver, their mother and father or whoever provides for their comfort and well-being. Caregivers help them develop trust, and then love develops from that trust.

When going through flight training, I was taught to trust my instruments. I was told that failure to trust my instruments could result in a tragedy. The same is true in loving relationships; if we don't have trust, we won't have a loving relationship. It's interesting how many aspects of youth are repeated in old age. If we don't trust our children to perform to our expectations and constantly do things for them, they will not develop into healthy adults. They will lose faith in themselves and their abilities and live a life of dependence. If we do not trust the elderly, they soon lose trust in their own abilities and will lose pride in accomplishments, just like children.

While returning from a recent vacation to Florida, Mary and I chose to let our car's GPS guide us home. It was not long before we began to distrust the route we were being directed to.

"This is not right," I said. "Where are they taking us?"

Both of us began to question our electronic guidance system. We did a couple U-turns before deciding to follow the obviously mistaken route our system provided. After a few miles, we began to regain trust, as it seemed we were finally going in the direction of home, at least. The highway we were on had less traffic and bypassed several large cities. We finally accepted that our navigational guidance was trustworthy.

A friend hired a well-regarded stonemason to build a stone wall along his driveway. It was not long before my friend was trying to choose the next rock to be placed in the wall. The stonemason did not appreciate the well-meaning advice. If you hire someone, you should let them do their work, or you will soon have a mess.

I remember an older man years ago saying loudly and with authority that he didn't have high blood pressure. His doctor didn't know his body like he did, and he was not going to take the medication the doctor prescribed. "I know how I feel when my pressure is up," he said, "and I know it is not up now." The next week, I read that the gentleman had died. I discovered later it was from a stroke. I wonder why we pay trained physicians and then do not follow their guidance?

Christianity is putting trust in Jesus and the Holy Spirit by listening to their guidance. Once we accept Jesus, we need to follow him through the Holy Spirit and trust the directions he gives us to live our lives. When we say, "Jesus, take my life, lead me home, and here is the direction I want you to take me," we are asking for a tragic ending. Loving Jesus requires trust.

Why is Christianity the best way? It is very simple: living a life of distrust is living a life without love. Christianity is love, and love is based upon trust. My pastor's sermon on Mother's Day included a thought that we Christians should be the most fearless people in the world because of the support of our Lord Jesus and the foundation and guidance he provides.

How wonderful it feels to believe the words of Jesus and the security those words promise each of us. Jesus used the parable of the mustard seed to explain that although Christianity had very small beginnings, it would grow into a worldwide community of believers. When we feel alone in our stand for Christ, realize that God is building a worldwide Kingdom. He has faithful followers in every part of the world, and your faith, no matter how small, can join with that of others to accomplish great things.

"Jesus asked. "How can I describe the Kingdom of God? What story should I use to illustrate it? It is like a tiny mustard seed. Though this is one of the smallest of seeds, it grows to become one of the largest of plants, with long branches where birds can come and find shelter.

"He used many such stories and illustrations to teach the people as much as they were able to understand. In fact, in his public teaching he taught only with parables, but afterward when he was alone with his disciples, he explained the meaning to them" (Mark 4:30–34).

"And he asked them, 'Why are you so afraid? Do you still not have faith in me?'" (Mark 4:40).

1. Did you feel fear when you gave your child the car keys for the first time?
2. Do you ever tell God how you want him to do things instead of asking him what he would have you do? Is that somewhat like telling your GPS which highway to use?
3. Do you listen to your physician and follow his or her advice? Do you listen closely to Jesus?
4. Do you have trouble trusting people you hire?

5. Did your parents tell you to call them anytime you got into trouble, no matter how bad it seemed? Isn't that the same advice Jesus gave us?

I never knew of a great painting that was created by two artists; however, others created the paint, canvas, brushes, and perhaps the inspiration.

Why Bother?

Question: Can you think of a time in your life when you asked the question, "Why am I doing this?"

Sometimes, your parenting, work, charity work, music, going to church, trying to live a Christian life, teaching, and dieting doesn't seem to be working.

I would venture to say that we've all asked that question to ourselves, if only in a perfunctory way. We sometimes become discouraged when the world doesn't respond to us in the way we want. If you're a parent, you may sometimes wonder why you worked so hard to provide when no one seems to appreciate your efforts. If you're a schoolteacher, you may become discouraged when the students don't seem to be listening despite your efforts. Physicians can get frustrated when they do everything in their power to help patients who don't comply. Pastors become discouraged when no one seems to make their Christian walk a bit more in harmony with God's love. This old world just doesn't seem to understand and respond as we would have it.

How many of us would like to have the opportunity to tell an old teacher or pastor how much they influenced our lives in a positive way? Do you ever offer a little prayer to your mother or father or someone who helped you, telling them you're sorry you didn't appreciate them when they were alive? How about prayers to your God, offering an apology and a thank you?

Many of us become discouraged when we try to diet but don't lose weight. Some people do everything expected to maintain health but despite their efforts, they develop a life-threatening illness. When Jacqueline Kennedy

Onassis was informed she had non-Hodgkin's lymphoma, she responded, "Why did I do all those sit-ups? Why did I bother?"

We pray and go to church, try to live a life of virtue, but think our prayers are unanswered. Why do we bother? Why don't we just do whatever we want? Stay home on Sunday, skip the prayers, eat what we want, have sex with whoever and whenever? Why not cheat, lie, steal, be slovenly, live a life just to feed our appetites, because it doesn't seem to matter? We observe others who live their lives in that manner and seem to have a wonderful life. When we Christians try to witness to nonbelievers, we often hear, "Why? All those people over there in your church live just like me, but they are not honest. Why, even that preacher you used to have ran off with his secretary."

Okay, here is the answer. Are you ready? The world is a dangerous place. There is evil in this world. God gave us this wonderful life and set us free to make our own decisions about how to live it. The reason he gave us the freedom to make decisions is so we can learn that a life of love and caring for God is the best life. Hopefully, we learn in this life that when we live a life of love for ourselves, our neighbors, as well as our natural surroundings, we show love for the Father. God knows that we will become discouraged on occasion, but he asks us to trust him and to know he is always there at our side. We may become sick despite our best efforts and even die because there is danger in this world. God didn't tell us that we would be protected from all dangers. He just told us that he will be there with us during our suffering, discouragements, and failures. God suffers with us because he loves us unconditionally. I remember Dad telling me as a teenager that if I ever got into trouble, I could call him or Mom. I always remembered those words, and I also remember him standing by me when I was in trouble. Trouble didn't always go away, but it sure felt good having my parents there beside me after I made a bad choice.

God forgives us when we make mistakes, if we learn from our mistakes, admit our bad choices, and then seek to make amends. We all sin and fall short of God's desires, church people as well as non-church people. Pastors and laypeople may not always live lives of virtue, but God only forgives those who ask. When we have remorse, intend to try to improve, and ask God, he forgives and forgets. Just like many other aspects of our failure to be more like Jesus, we often forgive our neighbors but don't forget their transgressions.

If you want to face this dangerous old world alone, you can turn your back on God and try to go it alone because he gives you that choice. However, your life will not be as content and fulfilling if you make this choice. A life lived loving and forgiving others is the happiest life, believe me, and believe Jesus. Love while you can, forgive while you can, encourage while you can, be thankful while you can, because life is short—shorter for some than it is for others. We know that if we walk hand in hand in this life with Jesus, we will walk into the perfect life with him. But if you want to live this life mad, never forgiving, and not loving, have at it. It's your choice; you may not admit it, but it was God who gave you that choice and offers forgiveness through his grace. If you fail to learn to love, your life will be unhappy; a Christian life of love is truly more content, at the least, and joyful, at best.

"Well then, are we Jews better than others? No, not at all, for we have already shown that ALL people, whether Jews or Gentiles, are under the power of sin. As the Scriptures say,

"'No one is good—not even one. No one has real understanding, no one is seeking God. All have turned away from God; all have gone wrong. No one does good, not even one. Their talk is foul, like the stench from an open grave. Their speech is filled with lies. The poison of a deadly snake drips from their lips. Their mouths are full of cursing and bitterness. They are quick to commit murder. Wherever they go, destruction and misery follow them. They do not know what true peace is. They have no fear of God to restrain them.'

"Obviously, the law applies to those to whom it was given, for its purpose is to keep people from having excuses and to bring the entire world into judgment before God. For no one can ever be made right in God's sight by doing what his law commands. For the more we know God's law, the clearer it becomes that we aren't obeying it.

"But now God has shown us a different way of being right in his sight, not by obeying the law but by the way promised in the Scriptures long ago. We are made right in God's sight when we trust in Jesus Christ to take away our sins. And we all can be saved in this same way, no matter who we are or what we have done.

"For all have sinned; all fall short of God's glorious standard. Yet now God in his gracious kindness declares us not Guilty. He has done this through Christ Jesus, who has freed us by taking away our sins. For God sent Jesus to take the punishment for our sins and to satisfy God's anger against us. We are made right with God when we believe that Jesus shed his blood, sacrificing his life for us. God was being entirely fair and just when he did not punish those who sinned in former times. And he is entirely fair and just in this present time when he declares sinners to be right in his sight because they believe in Jesus" (Romans 3:9–26).

1. If we were able to disrespect our parents and not honor them is it easier to disrespect and not honor God?
2. Do you feel good when you see others fail?
3. Do you expect nothing bad to happen in this life if you trust God?
4. Would you prefer to face danger alone? Would you want your children to face danger alone?
5. Do you always expect recognition and praise for doing your job?
6. Have you ever resented someone else who got recognition for your deeds?
7. Do you think you could offer a little more praise and a little less criticism of others?

THERE IS AN INTELLIGENCE OF A SUPREME NATURE, SUPPORTED BY LOVE IN EVERY CELL OF OUR BODY. LEARNING TO LISTEN TO THE VOICE EMANATING FROM IT IS WHY WE EXIST.